Switch Reference
in Koasati Discourse

Summer Institute of Linguistics and
The University of Texas at Arlington
Publications in Linguistics

Publication 109

Editors

Donald A. Burquest
University of Texas
at Arlington

William R. Merrifield
Summer Institute of
Linguistics

Assistant Editors

Rhonda L. Hartell

Marilyn A. Mayers

Consulting Editors

Doris A. Bartholomew
Pamela M. Bendor-Samuel
Desmond C. Derbyshire
Robert A. Dooley
Jerold A. Edmondson

Austin Hale
Robert E. Longacre
Eugene E. Loos
Kenneth L. Pike
Viola G. Waterhouse

Switch Reference
in Koasati Discourse

David P. Rising

A Publication of
The Summer Institute of Linguistics
and
The University of Texas at Arlington
1992

©1992 by the Summer Institute of Linguistics, Inc.
Library of Congress Catalog No.: 92-80355
ISBN: 0-88312-813-6
ISSN: 1040-0850

All Rights Reserved

No part of this publication may be reproduced, stored in a retrieval system, or transmitted in any form or by any means—electronic, mechanical, photocopy, recording, or otherwise—without the express permission of the Summer Institute of Linguistics, with the exception of brief excerpts in journal articles or reviews.

Cover design by Hazel Shorey
Adapted from a native basketry pattern

Copies of this and other publications of the Summer Institute of Linguistics may be obtained from

International Academic Bookstore
Summer Institute of Linguistics
7500 W. Camp Wisdom Road
Dallas, TX   75236

Contents

Abbreviations vii

Preface ix

Acknowledgments xi

1 Overview of the Problem and the Solution 1
   1.1 The phenomenon of switch reference 3
   1.2 Problems in the switch reference account 5
      1.2.1. Exceptional marking on verbs 5
      1.2.2. Distribution of the markers 5
      1.2.3. The larger set of markers containing -k and -n 9
      1.2.4. Conclusion 10
   1.3 Frequency of occurrence of some SR markers 11
   1.4 A functional approach 13
   1.5 Outline of this book 14

2 Sociolinguistics and Orthography 15
   2.1 A sketch of Koasati social and linguistic conditions 15
   2.2 Orthographic matters 17
      2.2.1. Sketch of Koasati phonemes 17
      2.2.2 Morphophonemics 18
      2.2.3 The syllable -ka 19

3 Some Relevant Features of Koasati Grammar 21
3.1 The nature of the rules governing SR 22
3.2 Some fundamental features of Koasati 23
   3.2.1. Parts of speech in Koasati 23
   3.2.2. Subject in Koasati 26
   3.2.3. Verbal morphology 27
   3.2.4. Active and stative verbs 28
   3.2.5. Koasati verbal chains 32

4 Koasati Continuity Marking 41
4.1 -*k* and -*n* on nouns: Markers of information type 41
   4.1.1. New information marked by -*n* in object slot 42
   4.1.2. New information marked by -*n* in subject slot 44
   4.1.3. Old information marked by -*k* in object slot 48
   4.1.4. Relationship of case and information flow 49
4.2 -*k* and -*n* on verbs: Markers of ±CONT 50
   4.2.1. Linking -*k* and -*n* to ommi 50
   4.2.2. Anomalous -*k* and -*n* between verbs 53
4.3 -*k* and -*n* on nouns and verbs in terms of ±CONT 56
4.4 Conclusion 58

5 Spectrum, -*Fooka*, and Switch Reference 59
5.1 The concept of spectrum and -*fooka* 59
   5.1.1. The concept of spectrum 59
   5.1.2. Morphology and semantics of -*fooka* 62
5.2 The discourse function of -*fooka*: Spectrum 65
   5.2.1. A Koasati text 65
   5.2.2. A translation indicating spectrum 68
   5.2.3. Discussion of text 69
5.3 ±CONT marking and -*fooka* 70
5.4 Some reflections 76
5.5 Counter-examples 77
5.6 Conclusion 78

References 79

Index 85

Abbreviations

ACC	accusative	NARRA	narrative suffix
ASP	aspect	NEG	negative
AUX	auxiliary	NOM	nominative
CAUS	causative	OBL	oblique
CLFT	cleft	OFFLIN	offline
CONJ	conjunction	PL	plural
CONN	connective	POS	possessive
±CONT	continuity/discontinuity	PRO	pronoun
DBLT	doublet, verb	PST	past
DELAY	delayed imperative	RDLOC	right dislocation
DIM	diminutive	REAL	realis
DIR	directional	RECIP	reciprocal
DIST	distal	SER	series
DO	direct object	SG	singular
DPST	distant past	SS	same subject
DS	different subject	STAT	stative
DU	dual	TAG	tag question
DUB	dubitative	TNS	tense
FRUS	frustration	TRNSL	translocative
FUT	future	VIA	action with intervening modification
HRSY	hearsay		
HUM	human	XR	cross-reference
ILL	illative		
INST	instrumental	1	first person
INTN	intention	2	second person
IO	indirect object	2om	link to *ommi*
IRR	irrealis	3	third person
LOC	locative		

Preface

Koasati, a Muskogean language, has long been classified as a switch reference language, but the function of the markers which constitute the system has not been fully studied and problematic phenomena have not been accounted for. The Koasati switch reference markers are found on both nouns and verbs which has led, variously, to the view that the markers are fulfilling two different semantic functions (homophony). Furthermore there are frequent exceptional markings in which rules of canonical switch reference are not followed. In this study it is proposed that the underlying function of Koasati switch reference is to mark continuity on a discourse-pragmatic level. This analysis unifies the semantics of the markers and accounts for exceptional marking. The theory is illustrated with a study of the discourse marker *-fooka*.

Acknowledgments

This book is a revision of a master's thesis in linguistics submitted to the University of Texas in May of 1990. In the process of writing and rewriting, a long list of people guided me and offered their most helpful criticism. I would enthusiastically like to thank each of them.

I am indebted first of all to the members of my thesis committee, Shin Ja Hwang, Donald A. Burquest, Heather K. Hardy, and Robert E. Longacre. My special thanks go to my committee chairperson, Shin Ja Hwang, who deeply invested her time, patience, and careful scholarship in the oversight of my work as well as gave me much personal support. Special thanks also to Heather Hardy who, with her considerable knowledge of Muskogean languages, greatly influenced and improved the quality of this work. Drs. Longacre and Burquest also contributed very helpful criticisms, insights, and guidance, making the final product much more coherent and sound. More recently Dr. Thomas Payne of the University of Oregon gave incisive comments which further helped to shape this published version of my work.

I wish also to express my deep appreciation and warm feelings for the many Koasati people who guided my wife and me in language learning and text gathering. It is nearly invidious to single out any one individual, and yet we would like to give special thanks to Marian John, whose infinite patience and integrity were a personal inspiration as well as being linguistically helpful.

Our field studies were carried out with the North America Branch of the Summer Institute of Linguistics. My family and I moved to Elton, Louisiana in 1985 and joined Gene and Martha Burnham as a second team. Gene greatly aided and guided us in language and culture learning and in building relationships. He also shared many texts the use of which has greatly enriched this work. I also wish to thank another SIL colleague, Wayne Leman, for his gentle and erudite guidance which made possible fundamental insights which led to chapters four and five. I gratefully acknowledge the assistance of Geoffrey Kimball of Tulane University who kindly provided Gene Burnham and me with copies of his Koasati word list and his dissertation.

All of the above greatly influence the final form of this work; I claim sole responsibility for errors and shortcomings which remain.

A number of other individuals contributed significantly through direct or indirect involvement with the production of this volume. Working and writing side by side with Phil Campbell was a great inspiration and benefit. My warm thanks to my family who supported me and endured my frequent absences from the home. Their spirit was exemplified by Laura (13) who, after observing the "n-th" revision and late night of work, asked with obvious empathy, "Dad, how many pages is it going to be, and how long will it take?"

1
Overview of the Problem and the Solution

Growing up in central California I spent much time in the Sierras among the magnificent giant sequoia trees. My cousin, Bill, and I often camped near some old groves and on one occasion found some ready firewood near a tree which had been cut up. We took some wood and bark and brought them back to camp. Later, returning wet and cold from hunting, Bill worked on breakfast while I set about getting a fire started.

The bark was dry and flaky, almost like shredded wheat, and showed promise of igniting easily. I split and arranged it like a good boy scout, smallest first, with a piece of paper placed underneath, struck a match, held it to the paper, and waited for the wood to catch fire. The paper burnt out leaving the bark unscathed. Somewhat surprised, I went through the operation a second time. Same effect. A few of the finest strands of bark burnt weakly, glowed, and fizzled out. Abandoning less civilized strategies, I doused the bark with some gasoline and tossed on a match! This produced an impressive fire but as soon as the gas was consumed, the fire went out.

At the time all this did not make a deep impression. I commented to Bill that the bark would not burn but, being intent on getting warm, went about making a fire with twigs and dry branches and the wood. I left the mystery as residue.

I have not lost my awe of the giant sequoias and on a recent vacation delighted in showing them to my children. On this trip I purchased a book about the trees and finally found out why I had not been able to start that fire years earlier: the bark is essentially nonflammable. The outer layer of bark of most trees consists of useless dead cells which happen to be flammable. In the case of the sequoia, the bark is an integral part of the tree and a shield of life, protecting the trees from forest fires, part of the natural ecology of the Sierras. In fact the sequoia is dependent upon fire for survival insofar as the seeds of the tree normally do not germinate unless a fire has passed through and prepared the needed soil and lighting conditions for the survival of seedlings.

Various characteristics of the bark hint at its significance. First of all is the one which I had noted as a teenager: it just won't burn. A second indication can be seen from diachronic observation. If a portion of bark is burnt away during a major fire, the tree quickly regenerates the bark and produces a buttress of protection against future fires and other threats.

This can be used as an illustration of the study of Koasati switch reference. Just as the bark of the sequoia has a role not apparent from cursory observation, so the various markers commonly referred to as SWITCH REFERENCE[1] markers have roles not easily perceived. Sequoia bark must be understood in terms of its function in the unusual and complex life cycle of the tree; Koasati switch reference must be understood in terms of its function and of the interrelationships of the whole grammatical system.

Like the bark, Koasati switch reference (hereafter SR) gives the observer various warning signs that there is more going on than canonical switching of reference. In the first place, it does not always "burn," i.e., it does not always switch when it should or it sometimes switches when it should not. Secondly, it metaphorically regenerates itself insofar as the SR markers occur essentially everywhere in the language.

In this work I attempt to describe the discourse function of the SR system of Koasati, a Muskogean language spoken primarily in Louisiana and Texas. I focus on three suffixes -*k*, -*n*, and -˜ (nasalization). The latter two, -*n* and -˜ , are closely related to one another; in this work the distinction between the two and the function of -˜ are discussed only briefly.[2] In linguistic analysis it can sometimes be said that the smaller they are, the harder they fall; Longacre (1977) refers to such small morphemes as

---

[1] The term SWITCH REFERENCE was first used by William Jacobsen, Jr. in his 1967 article.

[2] For the sake of brevity I do not always refer overtly to nasalization (˜) when listing or discussing the markers. Many statements applicable to -*n* may also be valid for -˜. This is not to imply that the markers have the same semantic range and function. In the examples, I follow the strategy taken by Hardy and Davis 1988 et al. and gloss *k*'s and *n*'s with the corresponding capital letter (K, N) rather than attempting to indicate the semantic value the morpheme might have in that particular occurrence. The same is true for *h* and *o* (H, O). This is discussed further in chapter four.

Overview of the Problem and the Solution

"mystery particles," and Grimes (1975) calls them "pesky little particles." These two morphemes play no minor and no transparent role in the grammatical system of Koasati. Kimball (1985:445) comments that "the importance of switch reference in Koasati cannot be underestimated [*sic*: read overestimated[3]];... Further study can only help to fill in the details of this important syntactic system." Indeed, SR is the warp and the woof of the language, the mortar which holds the whole building together.

One of the difficulties in arriving at a satisfactory analysis of the SR markers is their phonological size and the similarity of their phonological manifestation in free speech. In normal speech -*k*, -*t*, and -*p* occur in the identical environment and are realized in an unreleased form and so liable to be confused with one another. Nasalization is not always pronounced, as noted by Kimball who states that:

> the accusative suffix -*n* has a frequent allmorph, $\emptyset$. This is used in contexts where word order alone is sufficient to indicate that the noun is the object of the verb.[4] (1985:335)

In the balance of this introductory chapter, I have four purposes. In §1.1 I describe the phenomenon of canonical switch reference. I then illustrate the difficulties which -*k* and -*n* present to a standard switch reference interpretation. To get a feel for the phenomenon of SR in Koasati, I next give some statistical information on the frequency of occurrence of some of the markers. In §1.4 I describe the functional approach taken in this work, and in the final section outline the remaining chapters of this book.

1.1 The phenomenon of switch reference

Haiman and Munro (1983:ix) define canonical SR as:

> an inflectional category of the verb, which indicates whether or not its subject is identical with the subject of some other verb ... an affix on the verb indicates something about the identity of a noun.

In its simplest form, SR works like a TOGGLE SWITCH tracing subject between verbs. Or one could describe the switch referencing process in its simplest form as a functional substitute for pronouns in their canonical use

---

[3]This appears as "underestimated" in the original, but "overestimated" is almost certainly intended.

[4]Kimball's observation about the phonological patterns is well taken, but I will suggest that -*n* has functions other than as an "accusative suffix."

(Givón 1983b). Let us illustrate this with an example. Assuming that George and Sue had been introduced earlier, the following is a normal English sentence:

(1) **He** got dressed and ∅ went fishing, and **she** took a nap.

Koasati would produce this sentence without pronouns. Example (2) is in a hybrid form with English vocabulary and Koasati syntax. SAME and DIFF are the SR markers.

(2) get^dressed-SAME   go^fish-DIFF   take^nap

A Koasati speaker listening to the corresponding Koasati sentence would leave the toggle alone when they heard the marker SAME and hence would expect that the subject of the next[5] verb would be the same as the subject of the verb on which the marker occurs. However, upon encountering DIFF he or she would flip the toggle and expect a new subject or, as I shall argue, at least something new or different or discontinuous in what follows. The next examples illustrate how the system works.

(3) *Joekak roomkā itcokhalihkok Edkā hihcok cokko:lit*
     Joe-k room-˜ itcokhali:ka-k Ed-˜ hi:ca-k cokko:lit
     Joe-K room-˜ enter-K   Ed-˜ see-K   sat^down[6]
     Joe came into the room, saw Ed, and sat down.

(4) *Joekak roomkā itcokhalihkok Edkā hihcan cokko:lit*
     Joe-k room-˜ itcokhali:ka-k Ed-˜ hi:ca-n cokko:lit
     Joe-K   room-˜ enter-K   Ed-˜ see-N   sat^down
     Joe came into the room, saw Ed, and he [Ed] sat down.

(5) *Joekak roomkā itcokhali:kon Edkak hihcan cokko:lit*
     Joe-k room-˜ itcokhali:ka-n Ed-k   hi:ca-n cokko:lit
     Joe-K   room-˜ enter-N   Ed-K   see-N   sat^down
     Joe came into the room, Ed saw him, and Joe sat down.

---

[5]The matter is oversimplified here. Haiman and Munro 1983 "identify the clause in which switch-reference is marked as the marking clause, and the clause with reference to which it is marked as the reference clause" (see also Munro 1980a). In fact, in tracing SR in Koasati the order of the verbs is not always crucial. That is, the reference clause can precede the marking clause under various circumstances. Haiman and Munro (1983:xv, in footnote) observe that this also occurs in Pima and Papago.

[6]In order to ease reading, interlinear glossing is done in varying degrees of detail depending on the need of the point being illustrated.

Overview of the Problem and the Solution 5

Sentences (3) and (4) are a minimal pair, differing only in the marking on the verb *hi*ca*.[7, 8] In (3) there are no subject changes (all *-k*'s). In (4) there is one subject switch encoded by the *-n* on *hi:ca*. In (5) there are two subject switches; this is clumsy in English and would probably be reformulated, perhaps as, 'Joe came into the room and sat down, after Ed had seen him'. Participant tracing is transparent in Koasati: the toggles guide the listener. These sentences illustrate SR in its simplest form and present persuasive evidence for the validity of the canonical SR analysis.

1.2 Problems in the switch reference account

1.2.1. Exceptional marking on verbs. Using only the toggling model, one can march through a Koasati text elegantly dealing with the data. But eventually one encounters instances when the system should have switched and it didn't or when it switches and it should not have. Low level syntactic (internal) rules relating to subject switch are able to account for over ninety percent of the occurrences of SR in Koasati. But what of the roughly five or six percent exceptions? In subsequent chapters I discuss such anomalous examples, so no examples are presented here. For now, I outline other areas of difficulty.

1.2.2. Distribution of the markers. As quoted above, Haiman and Munro (1983:ix) describe "switch reference [as] an inflectional category of the *verb* [emphasis added]"; but the markers *-k* and *-n* (and others) occur on nearly any and every word in the language.[9] This feature has been

---

[7]The asterisk marks a location at which infixes and suffixes are obligatorily added. For example, the conjunction *ma*mi** requires both an infix and a suffix resulting in the following forms: *ma:mok, ma:min, mahmok, mahmin,* and *ma:mip*. Since this asterisk never occurs word initially it is not confused with the asterisk commonly used to indicate ungrammatical forms. This symbol is also used to mark the location of an infix in interlinear glossing (see example (27)). This method is called the "trace" method as in a*c-b (for root ac with infix b at position *). For more on this convention see Simons and Versaw (1988:2–21, 28).

[8]The verb *hi:ca* occurs in three (or more) forms (as do most Koasati verbs): *hi:ca, hihca,* and *hica*. The alteration of these infixes does have implications for the discourse connectedness/continuity of these verbs and is somewhat related to the function of the markers *-k* and *-n*, but cannot be further discussed within the limitations of this work.

[9]Compare Jones 1986:306 who states that "the difficulty in characterizing the semantics of *o-* arises partially from the fact that it occurs with all categories of words, as well as with phrases."

noted in all Muskogean languages by scores of linguists.[10] The phenomenon occurred in examples (3)–(5) above: the arguments *Joe* and *Ed* are marked variously with *-k* and *-n*. In the next example every word is suffixed with *-k* or *-n*—there are eleven words and eleven *-k/-n*'s.

(6)   *Canadakafo-n   acaffaaka-k   mathokotohno-n   conferenceko-n*
      Canada^LOC-N   be^one^time-K   they^send^us-N   conference-N

   amahilkatoho-k   ohtistilkahcooli-k   komistilka-k
   we^went-K   to^there^we^dwell-K   our^dwelling-K

   dormkooli-k   aabo-n   istilkahcooli-k[11] *mafã*
   dorm-K   upstairs-N   we^were^living-K   there-˜

Once we were sent to a conference in Canada; we went there and stayed and we lived in dorms—we were living upstairs there.

At first blush *-k* and *-n* on nouns look like case markers and have generally been so described.[12] However, getting back to the analogy, this

---

[10]Byington (in 1870 referred to in Todd 1975, Davies 1981 and 1982); Todd 1975; Heath 1977; Nathan 1980:44; Davies 1981 and 1982; Kimball 1985:195, 456; Schuetze-Coburn 1987 and many others. The anomalous behavior of the SR markers in Alabama, closely related to Koasati, has been a motivating interest in several articles jointly authored by Davis and Hardy (1984, 1985, 1987, and especially 1988, and Hardy and Davis 1988). My colleague, Gene Burnham of the Summer Institute of Linguistics, has often commented about unexplained SR marking in Koasati (p.c.).

Researchers have also wrestled with sometimes surprisingly similar phenomena in non-Muskogean languages such as Yavapai (Kendall 1975), Kiowa (Watkins 1978 and 1987), Kwtsaan (Slater 1977), Maricopa (Gordon 1983), Huichol (Comrie 1983), and Mbya Guarani in Brazil (Dooley 1989).

[11]Kimball 1985:143, 180–2 lists a tense marking suffix *-ki* which he glosses as PAST IV which has a word final form [-k] which is phonetically indistinguishable from the SR marker *-k*. It may be that the *-k* which occurs here on *istilkahcooli** is this tense marker rather than SR marking, but I am unable to adjudicate the question. In my data there are no occurrences of the form *-ki* (i.e., with the /i/), but language consultants sometimes do gloss sentence-final *k*'s as temporal. This analysis of *-ki* is supported by the parallel fact that the common past tense marker *-to* (PAST III in Kimball 1985:143) sometimes has a word final phonetic form [t] which is phonetically indistinguishable from SR *-t*. Unlike the situation with *-ki*, collocational and distributional patterns enable the listener to distinguish [t] derived from *-to* from [t] derived from SR *-t*. In the rest of this work the distinction between *-ki* and *-k* will not be made. I gloss *-to* simply as PST.

[12]See for instance Kimball 1985:332–6, as well as many other linguists who have worked in Muskogean languages.

Overview of the Problem and the Solution

description does not always "burn": -*k*'s sometimes occur on objects and -*n*'s sometimes on subjects.[13]

The markers -*n* and -˜ occur in wider distribution and with more diverse semantics than -*k*. Some of this diversity is shown in the next example.

(7)
1	2	3
stoklon	*matcimtohnollahō*	*ma:min*
stoklo-n	*matcimtohnoli-lahō*	*ma:mi-n*
be^two-N	I^send^to^you-FUT	CONJ-N

4	5	6
piłafã	*ohyã*	*matałī*
piła-fa-˜	*ohya-˜*	*matałi-˜*
boat-LOC-˜	be^all-˜	load^up-DELAY

I will send both to you and you load them all up (when they arrive).

All six words in example (7) are marked phonetically with either -*n* or -˜. A discussion of each marker follows.

1. -*n* at location 1 is marking the verb *stoklo* 'be two' as an oblique argument of the verb 'send'. This -*n* also illustrates that the markers appear with similar semantics equally on nouns and verbs. The Koasati word *stoklo* 'be two' is a verb but here is used in what one would tend to view as a nominal role. It is debatable whether the gloss of this -*n* should be DS or OBL, i.e., should be seen as marking switch reference or case.
2. The -˜ at locations 2 and 6 are not marking SR: -˜ at location 2 is part of the future suffix -*lahō*, and -˜ at location 6 is the delayed imperative.
3. -*n* at location 3 illustrates a SR marker on a conjunction: the subject of clause 1 'I will send' is different than that of clause 2 '(you) load!'.
4. -˜ at location 4 illustrates oblique marking on a locative: the cargo is to be loaded *onto* the boat.
5. -˜ at location 5 is similar to -*n* at location 1 insofar as *ohya* 'be all' here patterns as a noun/argument. The -˜ can be considered a case marker, marking the argument as the object of the verb 'load'.

SR marking also occurs on the deverbal conjunction *ma*mi** (location 3). Kimball (1985:456) observes that "There are a plethora of conjunctive

---
[13]Hardy and Davis (1988:216–7) and Davis and Hardy (1988:284–5, 288–9) have noted related phenomena in Alabama.

words in the language... These words relate the actions of the previous sentence to the following sentence in terms of sequence, dependence and causality. Additionally, nearly all of them are marked with switch-reference markers indicating whether the following sentence has the same or a different subject than the previous sentence."

Hence -*k* and -*n* function not only between verbs but also between clauses, sentences, and/or paragraphs.[14] This phenomenon is also illustrated in example (6) and throughout this work. Example (7) is a typical example of the role played by the Koasati SR markers which occur freely on virtually all words in the language.

The distribution of the markers has forced linguists to one of two solutions: (1) the diversity is due to the presence of homophones (markers of SR are homophonous with markers of case), or (2) there is an (as yet undiscovered) underlying semantic feature which unites the various functions of the SR markers. Kimball appears to take the view that we are dealing with homophony,[15] and Gordon (1987:66-7), working with Choctaw, states that "one set of switch-reference markers is homophonous with the case markers -*t* and nasalization..." and argues (1987:72) that "to account for the range of acceptable marking... of relative clauses in Choctaw, it is necessary to analyze them as marked either with SR or case-marking."

A similar situation obtains in Yavapai and Yuma which are non-Muskogean languages: here the main SR markers, -*k* and -*m*, are also used in ways suggesting the two separate phenomena of SR and case marking. But Kendall (1975:1) argues that:

> the likelihood of two morphemes being homophonous is therefore quite small... what is surely the case is that /k/ and /m/ are polysemous rather than homophonous, and that, whatever the semantic unities underlying their uses, they are far more abstract than has so far been recognized.

I concur with Kendall that we must search for the deep level notion which unites most of the -*k*'s and -*n*'s. I say "most" because -*n* is used in extremely diverse ways, making it seem unlikely that its semantics can be described under one rubric no matter how broad.

---

[14]Distinct linguistic units of clause, sentence, and paragraph are not all clearly represented in Koasati. This is discussed in chapters three and five below.

[15]My interpretation is based upon his statement that "it seems likely that originally they were unitary, nominal or nominalizing morphemes, which have become distinct from their distinctive uses" (1985:195).

1.2.3. The larger set of markers containing -*k* and -*n*.

-*k* and -*n* are members of a larger set of suffixes,[16] all of which contrast in the same word-final location and from which set members are obligatorily selected for use according to semantic needs. But this larger set does not constitute a set of SR markers: many members have no subject-tracing function whatsoever. It goes beyond the scope of this work to discuss this matter at length but a few illustrations will serve to support my contention. Note the following examples in which -*k* and -*p* contrast.

(8) *łoyohka-t   illa-k   akoyokpalaho*
    return^PL-CONN we^arrive-K   we^will^be^happy
    When we get back we will be happy.

(9) *łoyohka-t   illa-p   Sue-k cayahli-aahi-tik ommi-o-*⁻[17]
    return^PL-CONN we^arrive-P   Sue-K walk-INTN-but   AUX-O-IRR
    By the time we get back Sue will be walking, I imagine.

The semantics of the morpheme *p* are diverse and little understood; one of its meanings includes the irrealis connotation seen here. For my purposes note that in (9) *p* has displaced -*k*. But *p* is not a SR marker—it occurs with both DS conditions (seen in (9)) and SS conditions (seen in (10)).

(10) *toknawa:ci-li-p   anałłi-li-lahō*
     make^money-1^SG^XR-P   get^married-1^SG^XR-FUT
     If I make some money I'll get married.

Hence -*p* neutralizes the (assumed) switch-referencing function of -*k*. The suffix -*p* also replaces -*k* and -*n* on nouns and thus nullifies the assumed case-marking function of the two morphemes as can be seen in the next examples.

---

[16]All Muskogean languages have such a larger set of markers from which (supposed) SR markers are selected. Davis and Hardy 1988 describe the function of the three cognate Alabama markers -*t*, -*k*, and -*n* on a scale of "central" to "peripheral" and also include discussion of ∅ 'absence of noun marking' in terms of this same scale. Linker 1987 states that there are three sets of SR markers in Choctaw. A fruitful area of research would be a cross-Muskogean study of this set of markers. See also footnote 19.

[17]This use of nasalization (here glossed IRR) I do not view as being related to SR. The complex *ommō* following a verb with the suffix -*k* marks an irrealis condition which can be variously glossed 'I guess', 'it appears', etc. Similarly, on the preceding word a suffix -*tik* occurs which ends in a *k* which is not the ±CONT marker.

(11) ana-p   naaso-k   t:ammi-n ha:lo-li-k   acã
    1ˆSGˆPRO-P something-K fall-N   hear-1ˆSGˆXR-K outside
    I and I alone heard something fall outside.

(12) Johnka-k Catholicka-p anaɬɬakkohc
    John-K   Catholic-P   heˆdidˆnotˆ(wantˆto)ˆmarry
    At all costs John wanted to avoid marrying a Catholic.

In (11) -p marks a subject (most frequently marked by -k) and in (12) the same suffix marks an object (most frequently marked by -n or -˜). In both cases -p has been chosen not to mark the relationship of the argument to the verb (the realm of case) but rather to encode information about the argument to which it is attached. This use of -p I have called an ISOLATIVE use; it can be given the broad glossing 'of all the possible arguments this one alone'.[18] Furthermore, there are several other morphemes[19] which neutralize switch referencing (participant tracking) and case marking in favor of other notions.

1.2.4. Conclusion. What can all of this mean? In §1.2 I have outlined three areas of difficulty for a standard theory of SR. In the first place the markers -k and -n are sometimes anomalous. Secondly, traditional SR occurs on verbs and traces participants, but Koasati switch reference occurs on nearly all words and does so with an array of semantic functions. Finally, -k and -n can be omitted from a sentence leaving the listener to trace subject without SR or to determine case without case marking. (Which is not to say that such sentences are ambiguous, but to indict the view that -k and -n are necessary for tracing subject and object.)

These observations militate against the interpretation that we are dealing with a switch reference or case system at all and call for the analysis with an underlying principle which unites the function of all -k's and -n's as Kendall suggested. The solution offered here is one of discourse-pragmatic CONTINUITY.

---

[18]Note how dissimilar the semantics of this -p on a noun is to that above on a verb. I have been unable to find a common semantic feature which unites these uses.

[19]Other suffixes which in some sense replace -k and -n are: -t, -sa, -tik, -∅, -w, and DEL. Kimball 1985 uses DEL to refer to the common Koasati phenomenon of word final vowel loss. See also footnote 16.

Overview of the Problem and the Solution

1.3 Frequency of occurrence of some SR markers

Statistics on the frequency of occurrence of four SR markers are given in tables (13)–(15). Brief information on the related marker *-t* is included because it occurs quite frequently; it will not be treated in this work.[20] All three of the texts are narrative discourses, with the sermon text including hortatory sections. (The names of the texts are taken from my computer file names.)

In (13) the number 30 in the column "percent of text size" means that the marker *-k* occurs on 30% of the words in the text. The total for that same column, 86, indicates that 86% of the words in this text were marked by one of the four markers counted. In the rightmost column, 45 means that *-k* comprised 45% of the markers which occurred in this text, making it twice as common as the next most frequently occurring marker, *-n*. This ratio of 2 to 1 for *-k* and *-n* is fairly consistent in Koasati texts.

(13)   Frequencies in text *ser3noah* (text size: 244 words)

SR marker	Number of occurrences	Percent of text size	Percent relative to other markers
-t	34	14	21
-k	73	30	45
-n	38	16	23
-˜	18	7	11
Totals	163	**86**	**100**

---

[20]Briefly, *-t* marks the highest degree of CONTINUITY of all the Koasati SR markers. As such it is the easiest of all the markers to describe. It occurs on verbs connecting them in a very close relationship which, in my observation, is always SS. It also occurs on nouns marking them for subject or for series; the notion of series is a semantic function related to that just mentioned on verbs. In my data *-t* does not unambiguously mark any oblique case except in one (idiosyncratic?) use with the word Koasati as seen in the following example: *acayokp Koasati-t stannałihiska* 'I^am^glad Koasati-T you^spoke^to^me'. The suffix is similar to *-t* in Alabama described by Hardy and Davis 1988:290, 291, 294. As mentioned in footnote 11, this *-t* is not to be confused with the past tense marker *-to* which often occurs in shortened and homophonous form [t].

(14) Frequencies in text *gregfal* (text size: 194 words)

SR marker	Number of occurrences	Percent of text size	Percent relative to other markers
-t	15	8	10
-k	77	40	52
-n	37	19	25
-~	18	9	12
Totals	147	**86**	99

(15) Frequencies in text *roma* (text size: 305 words)

SR marker	Number of occurrences	Percent of text size	Percent relative to other markers
-t	37	12	16
-k	109	36	47
-n	59	19	26
-~	26	9	11
Totals	231	**76**	100

Exceptional marking in the same three texts is indicated in the following table. I have only counted -*k*'s and -*n*'s and only on verbs; exceptional marking on nouns occurs with less frequency.

(16) Exceptional marking in three texts

Text name:	ser3noah	gregfall	roma
Text size (no. words)	244	194	305
Total no. -k and -n	111	114	168
Exceptional markings	8	7	5
Percent exceptions	7	6	3

The total number of occurrences of the markers -*k* and -*n* in the first text considered is 111. Of these, eight or about seven percent were exceptional.[21] Figures from the other texts are also seen.

---

[21]Regarding Alabama, related to Koasati, Hardy (p.c.) estimates that SR marking is canonical at least 80–90% of the time.

Overview of the Problem and the Solution

1.4 A functional approach

Givón (1983b:68–9) warns that we need to view the phenomenon of SR in light of the wider FUNCTIONAL domain of TOPIC CONTINUITY rather than from a narrow, STRUCTURAL[22] perspective.

> Traditionally, the term switch-reference has been applied almost exclusively to *subject*-switch... There is nothing wrong with this traditional practice *per se*, since the main vehicle of topic continuity in language is indeed the subject—or "main clausal topic." Therefore, the most interesting and functionally important topic-*discontinuity* in language is obviously that of *subject switching*. If one is interested in discovering the general principles—functional as well as coding principles—which govern the grammar of the SS/DS "canonical" distinction, then I think one is better off developing an overview of the entire functional domain of topic continuity in discourse, within which the "canonical" SS/DS contrast obviously plays an important part.

Givón argues that the phenomenon of SR is a subset of the universal functional domain of topic continuity. I shall attempt to show that most anomalous markings and most of the diverse semantic functions of the markers can be explained from a perspective of continuity marking. Consider the following illustration (in which the symbol ≤ means 'is a subset of'); the figures at the bottom of the chart are only approximate and are added to give a feel for the relative frequency of the semantic content of the Koasati SR markers.

(17) Relationships of subject and continuity

subject tracing ≤ topic continuity ≤ general continuity
90%　　　　　　　95%　　　　　　　100%

-*k* and -*n* always mark some kind of continuity or discontinuity. They usually mark subject reference. When -*k* and -*n* cannot be accounted for in terms of concepts on the left of the cline, this is due to higher allegiance to their functional role as CONTINUITY markers.

The Koasati SR markers -*k* and -*n* trace a broad concept of CONTINUITY-DISCONTINUITY. (Hereafter CONTINUITY and DISCONTINUITY will be abbreviated as +CONT and −CONT or, when both are to be signified, with

---

[22]See also 1983b:xv and 51.

±CONT.) Statistically the kind of ±CONT marked on verbs is usually that of subject, hence we have the concept of switch reference applied to the system. However, the ±CONT marking system also functions to mark a number of other notions such as causality, implication, sequencing, expectation, and various other discourse-pragmatic matters. I also show that the function of -*k* and -*n* which has been identified as case can also be subsumed under the category of ±CONT.

1.5 Outline of this book

The chapter immediately following deals with some practical matters: with first an outline of the sociolinguistic situation of Koasati in Louisiana, and secondly a description of the phonology of the language.

In chapter three the salient features of SR languages are addressed with an outline of some features of Koasati grammar and SR in order to investigate ±CONT marking against the broader backdrop of Koasati grammar.

The last two chapters comprise the main contributions of this work. Chapter four investigates different kinds of exceptional marking in Koasati discourse and explains these in terms of ±CONT marking. The last chapter deals with the use of the verbal suffix -*fooka* which functions on the level of discourse, establishing levels of information, and demonstrating that the ±CONT marking system is sensitive to these levels of information. This is an attempt to show that Koasati SR is not just a syntactic phenomenon but a pervasive system which interacts with high level features of texts.

2
Sociolinguistics and Orthography

2.1 A sketch of Koasati social and linguistic conditions

Koasati [kowasati] is the name used by the Koasati people and the academic community to refer to the tribe known legally and popularly as the Coushatta. The Koasati language is spoken by a little over 200 speakers living in the vicinity of Elton, Louisiana. A smaller group of speakers lives on the Alabama-Coushatta Indian Reservation near Livingston, Texas, along with approximately 600 members of the Alabama tribe.

In addition, a number of tribal members live outside these two main communities. In 1988 Loveland Pancho, the tribal chairman, kindly provided me with a list of tribal members which includes names of over 100 people living in various towns in Louisiana and Texas and in a few other states. It was not determined exactly how many individuals are thereby represented or how many of these use Koasati, although language use is probably less intense in these situations.[23]

Though significantly different, the closest linguistic relative of Koasati is the Alabama language spoken primarily on the Alabama-Coushatta Indian Reservation. A number of Indian people from both the Alabama and Koasati tribes who live in Texas speak both languages, and all Texas

---

[23]Nonetheless, the Koasati people are deeply committed to their language. One family lived abroad and in other states for decades, yet everyone in the family used Koasati exclusively in the home. When they returned to Elton, their speech form, retained in isolation, had undergone less diachronic change than the local expression, and the parents used vocabulary forgotten by Elton Koasati.

Alabamas transplanted to Louisiana speak Koasati. Language use is declining in both communities, but Koasati is the more sociolinguistically viable of the two, which is mentioned by members of both groups and can be observed by comparing language use in Elton with that in Livingston. Informal surveys and interviews with principals and kindergarten and first grade teachers in Elton and Livingston indicate that English is being used by more and more pupils. Comments from parents confirm this trend.

Until approximately 1975 language use in Elton, Louisiana was almost 100 percent. Children went to school speaking no English, and all age groups much preferred the use of Koasati even if fluent in both English and Koasati. The situation in the schools has changed radically since then, however. Kindergarten teachers in the Elton school district report that in the eight to ten years prior to our investigation (1988), all students spoke English well upon entering school and many could not speak Koasati at all. Younger girls are particularly reluctant to speak Koasati despite pressure from adults and boys.

I know of only two individuals who speak no English[24] and both of these are elderly. All elderly tribal members prefer their indigenous language, and speakers over thirty years of age resort to English only when addressing those who do not know the language, even if fluent in English. Language use is not to be understood in terms of diglossia, as bilinguals use both languages in all domains of language use. Rather, code switching is determined by this simple rule: If the other speaks Koasati then speak Koasati, if the other does not speak Koasati then speak English.[25] This code switching process is natural to Koasati speakers and is adhered to by all but the youngest speakers. One lady told me that she could not recollect ever having spoken English with her children.

It is unlikely that the decline in language use will halt. The community is, as noted, quite small, and in the last decade fewer Koasati to Koasati marriages have been occurring, a matter of concern to parents and some children. In the period from 1985 to 1989 only three children were born in Koasati speaking families in the Elton area. During the 1989 Christmas season my wife and I returned to Elton for a visit after an absence of twelve months. At a New Year's party with Koasati friends, we noted that

---

[24]It is noteworthy that one of these speaks both Choctaw and Cajun. Cajun is a dialect of French brought to Louisiana in the eighteenth century by French refugees displaced from Acadia (Canada). Several Koasati speak Cajun and some speak it better than they do English.

[25]Kimball 1985:487 states that "there is little interface between Koasati and English use among Koasati speakers. Koasati is used in all situations where another speaker is present, and English is used with non-Indians."

Sociolinguistics and Orthography

teenage boys had begun using English with girls and even with one another. This constitutes an accelerated and radical shift in language use.

Koasati will doubtless be spoken throughout the lifetime of tribal members who by now are in their twenties, due to a love for their indigenous language. Most older tribal members view their language as an important feature of their self-identity. Johnson (1976:50) comments that the language

> remains today as the distinguishing cultural mark that sets the Coushattas apart from other Indian people; therefore, the retention of the Coushatta tongue during the migration period was a major factor in the survival of their culture.

2.2 Orthographic matters

2.2.1. Sketch of Koasati phonemes. The Koasati phonemic inventory consists of three vowels with short and long forms and fourteen to sixteen consonants depending upon some theoretical matters which do not concern us here. The vowel phonemes are /i/, /a/, and /o/—front, low, and back vocoids respectively—with considerable etic variation. The consonants are listed in (18).[26] Nasalization (˜) and vowel and consonant length (:) also occur.

(18) Consonant phonemes of Koasati

	Labial	Alveolar	Alveopalatal	Velar	Glottal
Vl stops	p	t	c	k	
Vd stop	b				
Vl fricative	f	s			h
Lateral		l			
Lateral fricative		ł			
Nasals	m	n			
Glides	w		y		

The symbol *c* represents the alveopalatal grooved affricate.
The symbol *ł* represents the voiceless lateral fricative.

Neither nasalization nor length can be categorized as strict phonemes. Kimball (1985:29) refers to nasalization as a "marginal phoneme"; it occurs mainly with a grammatical function. In this work nasalization is viewed as

---

[26]The system is asymmetrical in that voiced stops /d/ and /g/ and voiced fricative /v/ are missing. For further details see Kimball 1985, chapter two.

one of the SR markers and is marked by a tilde (˜) over the vowel or, in the case of interlinear text, after the vowel concerned.

Length (:) has several functions in the phonology of the language, one of which is to mark contrastive vowel length. There are two kinds of vowel length, one which Kimball (1985) calls "genetic" and one which is "induced" by various means; in this work I refer to these as underlying and derived length. Underlying vowel length remains long regardless of conditions; for instance, *oo* in *foosi* 'bird' intrinsically occurs with length. Such vowel length in this work is marked VV rather than with V: in order to enhance our consciousness that there is also a derived kind of length (:) which is a phoneme (infix) meaningful on the level of the grammar and, partly, the lexicon.

Vowel length also occurs internal to verbs. Consider the verb *hi*ca* which occurs in three forms: *hi:ca*, *hihca*, and *hica*, depending upon factors related to aspect and discourse. The verb clearly occurs more frequently in the form with the vowel length; the form with *h-* infixed has been viewed as the Muskogean *h*-grade infix, and the form *hica* has not been described to my knowledge.[27] In order to facilitate perception of the infixation and switch referencing process I treat this length marked with a colon (:) as an infix which has been added to a root form *hi*ca*. This same symbol also marks grammatically and lexically induced consonant gemination such as seen in example (19).

(19)   (a) *sobaylil*   'I understand'
       (b) *sob:aylil* 'I remember'

In (b) the /b:/ is pronounced with a distinct pause and intensity typical of geminate stops and connotes an iconic lengthening of the semantics of (a).

A shortcoming in my data is the absence of accent marking. Early decisions about how to write the language were based upon considerations of a practical orthography and it was decided that pitch-accent would not have to be indicated. Kimball (1985:32–3 and elsewhere) notes that "location of pitch can distinguish between two items."

2.2.2 Morphophonemics. Morphemes are written in their underlying form; this is illustrated with the morpheme which marks third-person indirect object.

---

[27]One example is the loss of length in verbal doublets such as *bookkon hicak scokko:lit*, literally 'book see sat', free translation 'he sat looking at a book' or 'sitting he looked at a book'. Hardy and Montler's 1988 article examines similar data in Alabama.

Sociolinguistics and Orthography

(20) Orthographic convention for third-person indirect object

3^IO → [il] / _l
[im]/ _b, m, p, or vowel
[in] / _n, t
[iñ] / _c
[iŋ] / _k
[ĩ] / _fricatives (f, h, ɫ, s)
[iw]/ _w
[iy] / _y

Because this work focusses on discourse matters, this morpheme is written as *im*. Similar theoretical decisions are applied to other phenomena. For instance, when a suffix ending in /s/ precedes /hci/ the /h/ elides, producing phonetic [sci], but is written /shci/.

2.2.3 The syllable -*ka*. The syllable -*ka* is added to borrowed foreign words for phonotactic reasons and is not glossed in interlinear texts. Multisyllabic names have this syllable added (*Robertka*). Also consider these phrases heard when two young men were working on their car: *batteryka deadka* 'the battery is dead' and *seatka shove^backka* 'shove back the seat'.

3
Some Relevant Features of Koasati Grammar

One difficulty in analyzing Koasati SR is that the grammatical system of Koasati is strikingly unlike that of, say, English. The SR system is interrelated with the grammatical system so that SR cannot be approached without awareness of how the language functions as a whole. Davis and Hardy (1985:59) give an illustration which I apply to the idea that Koasati SR can only be understood in context:

> An appropriate metaphor would be the sorting of one's possessions into piles for disposal and for retention. Items in the "keep" pile may be sometimes valuable, but sometimes not; sometimes new and unused, but also worn; sometimes useful (tools and implements) but sometimes not. It would be difficult to examine the division and determine the rationale underlying assignment to one pile or the other. One has looked at roles in Choctaw and Chickasaw and seen no pattern because the kind of pattern expected is not the one that is present.

This chapter introduces some features of Koasati grammar which have implications for an understanding of SR. First, I reflect on the nature of the rules governing SR and then survey some relevant aspects of Koasati grammatical structure.

3.1 The nature of the rules governing SR

There are SR languages which are reportedly 100 percent regular and others with few exceptions. Olive Shell (p.c.) reports that with years of work in Cashibo, a South American Indian language of Amazonia, she never noted any exceptions in that language's SR system.

Dooley (1989) reports that Guarani, a SR language found in Brazil, is nearly 100 percent regular. In his article, Dooley focuses on the approximately one percent of the cases where Guarani SR marking shows some kind of exceptional marking. He (93–4) states that:

> "in most cases," switch reference signals sameness or difference of grammatical subject; but in exceptional circumstances, it signals sameness or difference of other kinds, involving semantic or pragmatic information that is different from grammatical subject reference.

It is noteworthy that in the few cases where the Guarani SR system is irregular, the anomalous data are accounted for with reference to a broad notion of SAME and DIFFERENT.

Dooley (101) introduces the useful notion of "subject set." The subject set of a particular verb consists of the set of referents which comprise the morphosyntactic subject of that verb. For example, in the sentence 'we went walking, and I saw a squirrel', the subject set of the second verb (I) is contained in the subject set of the first verb (we). Likewise 'Joe and Tom went walking, and Joe saw a squirrel'. Or there are disjoint subject sets in which the two subject sets share no common arguments; examples are trivial such as 'Tom went walking, and Joe saw a squirrel'. Guarani and Koasati also have verbs with empty subject sets, i.e., verbs which have no syntactic subject at all. Ambient verbs such as 'it's hot' and 'it's raining' would be examples from English. This is discussed further under stative verbs in §3.2.4.

Many so-called SR systems mark information other than SR. Besides the references listed in footnote 10 of chapter one, a sampling can be found in Haiman and Munro (1983) where, for instance, Comrie shows that subordination and dependence are marked in the SR system in Huichol, and Gordon demonstrates that in Maricopa the SR system is used to identify structures such as reason and purpose clauses.

It is misleading to lump all these systems under the one rubric of switch reference lest the nomenclature lead us to misperceive some of the dynamics of each system. Dooley and Shell (p.c.) both commented that the phenomenon of Koasati SR appears to be something significantly different than that found in Guarani and Cashibo respectively. Similarly Givón (1983b:51) warns against an approach to SR which is too "narrow—and thus rigorous" lest we "disregard important facts." One problem with the term switch reference (of subject) is that the name begs the question by implying that the markers comprising the system have a function which is restricted to the realm of syntax. Dooley (1989:94–5) discusses the nature of the description one is able to provide of the Guarani SR system:

> Consider a syntactic phenomenon which can be accounted for by means of a rule involving only grammatical features, such as grammatical subject, and another phenomenon which can be satisfactorily accounted for only if extragrammatical factors, such as the discourse-pragmatic notion of topic, are brought in. In Hyman's (1984) terms, the first phenomenon has an internal explanation, while the second calls for an external explanation.

Dooley accounts for exceptions with external explanations, as I do in Koasati.

However, the discourse structure of Koasati is not well understood, so we would do well to heed Watkins's (1987:324) words: "It is hard enough to make sense out of discourse elements in one's own language, let alone say anything intelligent about a language studied in a field context." This state of affairs forces me to choose language which is sometimes loose; such expressions can be found in Watkins' (319, emphasis added) article: "the utterance... bears *some* connection to the immediately preceding utterance ..." Such wording will, however, not always be strictly due to a shortcoming in our understanding of Koasati discourse; it is also partly due to the intrinsic nature of how SR marking signals meanings. As Watkins goes on to say, "The nature of that connection is *unspecified* and left to the interpretation of the addressee according to *general* conversational implicature."

3.2 Some fundamental features of Koasati

In this section I examine some basic structures of Koasati grammar which are relevant to the study of the ±CONT marking system. The subsections which follow are parts of speech in Koasati, subject in Koasati, verbal morphology, active and stative verbs, and chains.

3.2.1. Parts of speech in Koasati. The part of speech "adjective" does not exist in Koasati and the existence of adverbs is debatable.[28] Adjectives

---

[28] Kimball (1982 and 1985) appears to recognize adverbs as a class of words.

and adverbs are verbs whose functions are indicated by semantics, verb type, and by ±CONT marking. Some adverbial words are formed from verbs with *-k, -n, -p,* and others appended; other adverbial meanings are encoded by verbal morphology.

Kimball states that "there are [sic] a plethora of conjunctive words in the language." As he implies, it is misleading to refer to these words as CONJUNCTIONS because morphologically they are generally verbal in nature and functionally they do not always pattern like Indo-European conjunctions which mark diverse kinds of interclausal relations.[29] The ±CONT markers sometimes replace the role of conjunctions, and, vice versa, most Koasati conjunctions include or imply SR.

Concepts which one might naively expect to be expressed by nouns may be replaced by Koasati verbs:[30]

(21) *hatłi*   'he wears shoes'
      stiliofka   'he wears pants'
      a:sa   'he carries something in the arms'
      ilapacatłi:ci 'he carries something on the hip'
      cini:ka   'he carries something on the lower back'
      labanna:li   'he carries something on the shoulder'
      pa:pa   'he carries something on the upper back'

Words which express relationships sometimes look nominal but are verbal.

(22) ca-halki-k   ho:pahci
      1^SG^DO-wife-K be^sick
      My wife is sick.

(23) Maryk   acakkok   atiyato   Josephkā; yok
      Mary-k   acakko-k   ati:ya-to   Joseph-⁻; ya-o-k
      Mary-K   accompany-K travel-PST   Joseph-⁻   this-O-K

---

[29] Chaining languages in general may frequently have different means of marking interclausal relations. Longacre 1985a:276 reports of Wojokeso, a chaining language of Papua New Guinea, that "only one free conjunction occurs in the entire language." Compare Gordon 1983 who shows that SR marks "interclausal relationships" in Maricopa.

[30] Much of the information discussed here occurs also in Kimball's work. Adverbs occur as the first of fifteen levels of suffixes; see Kimball 1982 and 1985:140, 145–52. The status of numbers is noted also by Kimball 1985:299.

Josephkā halkaahik imfaykahcoto
Joseph-˜ halki-aahi-k im-fayka-hci-to
Joseph-˜ be^wife-FUT-K 3^IO-be^promised-ASP-PST
Mary was traveling with Joseph; she had been promised to him as wife (from the Christmas story in the Bible).

In (22) the word *halki* 'wife' would initially be perceived as a noun. In (23) the word is seen to be a verb, expressing a relationship and being marked for future tense. A similar example is in (24):

(24) *Josephkak Davidkā imalahkōto*
    Joseph-k David-˜ im-alahka-o-to
    Joseph-K to David 3^IO-be^related-O-PST
    Joseph was related to David.

Most affixes function equally on nouns and verbs, although there are affixes which occur specifically on one or the other.[31] Nouns can be marked for tense,[32] such as with *-toho* in (25).

(25) *casbakotohok amho:pak*
    ca-isbaki-o-toho-k am-ho:pa-k
    1^SG^DO-head-O-PST^REAL-K 1^SG^IO-hurt-K
    My head was hurting me.

The concern to classify Koasati words as nouns or verbs may in the final analysis be otiose. Schachter (1985:6) comments that "some rather celebrated questions—for example, whether or not all languages make a distinction between nouns and verbs—may ultimately turn out to be more a matter of terminology than of substance." In Koasati the distinction between nouns and verbs, if pushed too far, becomes more of a liability than an asset. Nouns are treated like verbs and, most important to discern, Koasati grammar functions mainly by virtue of its verbs and SR markers. The latter, appended to virtually every word, serve as the stationmaster and conductor, controlling and defining the function of each word; and each word is controlled or defined in roughly the same way, whether it be noun or verb.

---

[31]For instance, I have not observed the discourse level markers *-fooka* and *-hci* on nouns. Furthermore nouns are clearly not as heavily affixed as verbs.

[32]The exact purpose of this marking is not well understood. This particular example occurred in an extended discourse and any account of the function of the marking must be sought from that angle.

This is not to claim that nouns and verbs are morphologically identical—this would be incorrect—but rather, in the words of Schachter (1985:11–2, emphasis added), to say that nouns and verbs "show, from the point of view of a language like English, rather surprising similarities of *function* and *categorizations*." It is, however, essential for the present argument to blur the distinction between noun and verb in Koasati, because the conclusion I am aiming at is to unify the function of the ±CONT markers on nouns and verbs... indeed, on all words.

3.2.2. Subject in Koasati. Watkins (1978, 1987:319, cf. 1978:42) states that "subject is not a very useful notion in Kiowa" and finds that SR marking is concerned with "role." I likewise find that subject is not highly relevant to Koasati although the notion of role is not central to Koasati nor, perhaps, to any of the Muskogean languages (cf. Munro and Gordon 1982). An illustration of the kind of confusion which arises when we try to identify subjects is found in (26).

(26) *piła talibo:ci:fookon   oybak   i:la:fookow*
     piła talibo:li-ci-:fooka-n   oyba-k   i:la-:fooka-w
     boat make-2^SG^XR-OFFLIN-N rain-k? arrive-OFFLIN-W
     boat (when) you make   rain   (when) it comes

   stokpaka:laahitik...
   st-okpaka:li-aahi-tik
   INST-float-FUT^2-but
   [things] will float but

   After you make the boat, the rain, when it comes, [or it rains, when it comes] will float everything away but...

(27) *oykibō*
     oy-ki-ba-ō
     oy*ba-ki-ō
     be^rain-3^NEG-NEG
     It is not raining.

In (26) *oyba* 'rain' looks like a noun, but in (27) it is seen to be a verb with distinctly verbal negation marking (*-ki-* and *-ō*). Thus we ask whether in (26) *oyba* is a noun, and hence the *-k* is marking subject, or *oyba* is a verb and the *-k* is marking same subject?

As above in the discussion of noun versus verb, I do not wish to summarily throw out the word "subject," but we must avoid laying too great an emphasis upon subject tracing and marking. At this time I am unable to offer a rigorous definition, but to clarify my use of the term, by subject I will generally refer to the morphosyntactic subject or will clarify the usage where needed.

Let us return to the subject of pronouns and the broader domain of referential tracking. Two systems are widely used to trace participants in language: (1) verb agreement and (2) independent pronouns. To this list SR languages add a third system called switch reference.[33] In Koasati, first and second person are explictly marked in the verb, and SR marking works effectively to trace referents, so that independent personal pronouns rarely trace participants. In a statistical search of three texts totaling 743 words, only six pronouns traced participants and most of these were in a contrastive role, e.g., 'you do this but *I* will do this'. Again, a part of speech is somewhat replaced by verbal morphology.

Another way that the standard role of pronouns is obviated is by the use of verbs of number, for example, one finds the following verbs filling the function of the pronoun 'we': *stoliklo* 'we are two' (from *sto*klo* 'be two' plus *-li-* 1^PL^XR) and *olihya* 'we are all' (used to designate more than two, from *o*hya* 'be all' plus *-li-* 1^PL^XR).

(28) olihyak   kolohkaahosit
      o-li-hya-k   ko-lohka-aahosi-t
      o*hya-li-k   ko-lohka-aahosi-to
      be^all-1^PL^XR-K 1^PL^DO^STAT-be^tired-very-PST
      We were all tired out, every one of us.

In summary, Koasati sentences are mostly composed of verbs with elaborate SR marking.

3.2.3. Verbal morphology. All this makes for complex verbal morphology. Kimball (1985) outlines the morphology of the verb, listing nine levels of prefixes and fifteen levels of suffixes, with the SR markers occurring as the final layer of suffixation. He also lists various infixes including the pan-Muskogean grades; I have expanded this somewhat to include three levels of infixation, including a kind of ±CONT marking in the verb stem.[34]

---

[33]The argument is here over-simplified. Givón (1983b) points out that English has features of SR which are perhaps universally present in varying degrees in the languages of the world.

[34]The morphology of infixation is not discussed in this work. In a related vein, Kimball 1985:254 states that the "h-grade... is used to indicate that actions occur in a sequence..." It is this sequencing function of the h-grade infix that is related to ±CONT marking.

Kimball (1985:53) refers to the verbal conjugation patterns of Koasati as "elaborate." There are three major classes of affirmative nominative subject cross-reference markers with several subcategories of each depending, for the most part, on whether the markers occur as prefixes, infixes, or suffixes. Third person nominative is not cross-referenced on the verb, so when necessary, the zero marker is indicated with ∅; otherwise an absence of cross-reference marking can be assumed to indicate third person, either singular or plural. Gender is not indicated and number of third person arguments is shown only in some verb stems and inconsistently with a verbal prefix *ho-* (PL, DISTRIBUTIVE). For the most part, third person is not well marked on the verb so that the SR marking system is sometimes solely responsible for participant tracking in discourses involving multiple third-person arguments. As Haiman and Munro (1983:xi) observe:

> Whether or not switch-reference is indicated by verbal concord or a separate category, it is redundant where either subject is first or second person, and necessary where both subjects are third person.[35]

In order to better understand how ±CONT marking functions, I describe active and stative verbs in the language in the next subsection, and, in the section following that, the phenomenon of Koasati verbal chains.

3.2.4. Active and stative verbs. There is a common distinction in many languages between active and stative verbs. As a typological concept Schachter (1985:11) describes ACTIVE verbs as those "which express actions and the like" and STATIVE verbs as those "which express states and the like." This description is broadly descriptive of the phenomenon in Koasati, although the line between the two types of verbs is not always easily drawn. Hardy and Davis (1989:2–3) argue that the basis of the distinction between these two verb types in Alabama is best explained in terms of the "semantics of control" where control describes a system which is "similar in some respects to those that have been described for Salish and other language families." An element of control is found in Koasati as well, but in this work I describe the distinction between active and stative verbs in terms of volitionality and agency.

Morphologically, the main difference between active and stative verbs in Koasati is that the subjects of active and stative verbs are cross-referenced by different sets of markers. The subject of an active verb is cross-referenced by the nominative cross-reference marking set while the subject

---

[35]Strictly speaking, SR can be necessary in second-person forms as well, as when two persons are addressed ('you go there and you remain here').

Some Relevant Features of Koasati Grammar 29

of stative verbs by either the direct or indirect object pronominal cross-reference sets (there are two kinds of stative verbs). For the purposes of examining stative versus active verbs, the nominative markers can be viewed as a single set, sometimes referred to as Type I.[36] In this work the direct and indirect object markers are referred to as the *ca* set (Type II) and the *am* set (Type III) where *ca* and *am* are the first-person singular pronominal markers from each set. An impression of how the system works can be gotten from the following examples from English in which the grammatical categories of subject and object are reversed.

(29) I like cheese.   Corresponds to active
      Cheese tastes good to me.   Corresponds to stative

As in many languages, adjectival meanings in Koasati are communicated with verbs, specifically stative verbs. In addition to this, colors, qualities, numbers, and the like are expressed by stative verbs.

Stative verbs are also often employed when the subject of a verb is perceived to be not agentive or is perceived to be lacking in volition. In many instances when the subject is an EXPERIENCER of a verbal action it is cross-referenced on the verb as an object, but this is not always the case.[37]

The table in (30) gives a sample of verbs illustrating the distinction between active and stative verbs and, furthermore, between the two types of stative verbs found in Koasati. The majority of verbs are active, and *ca* stative verbs greatly outnumber *am* statives.

---

[36]The active set of agreement markers, which I here describe as unitary, actually consists of three separate sets of considerable morphological dissimilarity and there are, again, subsets of these three sets. And these are only the positive markers; there are also parallel sets of negative conjugation markers. Munro and Gordon (1982) first used the procedure of labeling the sets by numbers, and it has been adopted by other Muskogeanists such as Hardy and Davis (1989:5). See Munro 1983 for a fuller explanation of the procedure.

[37]Compare Foley and Van Valin 1980 who argue that Choctaw is a "role dominated" language and the response of Munro and Gordon 1982 who question this classification.

(30)

I	II		III	
active verbs	*ca* stative verbs (DO) (adjectives)		*am* stative verbs (IO)	
wali:ka 'run'	*aho:ta*	'vomit'	*sohbi*	'have blurry vision'
batapli 'hit'	*snookca:ka*	'choke'	*stinsalatli*	'slip'
hi:ca 'see'	*alotka*	'be full'	*achihba*	'be sad'
	ayokpa	'like someone'	*aya:ci*	'be distracted'
(most verbs	*sammi*	'be able'	*alosti*	'like something'
are in	*cahno*	'feel cold'	*campoli*	'like food'
this class)	*samohka*	'be numb'	*samohli:ci*	'feel tingle'
	smahmi	'feel better'		
	yimmi	'believe'		

Several stems appear in both columns II and III such as the verb *ho:pa*, seen below, which signifies a negative bodily state or experience.

(31)   *ca-ho:pa*
       1^SG^DO^STAT-be^sick
       I am sick.

(32)   *catołbi   am-ho:pa*
       my^knee 1^SG^IO^STAT-be^sick
       My knee hurts.

A further complication is that the division between active and stative is not unbridgeable. Known as fluid marking, almost any active verb can be treated as a stative verb[38] if the subject of the verb is perceived to be volition. The verb *nakałła* provides an example of a verb which occurs naturally in all three categories.

(33)   *nakałłal*
       nakałła-li
       nakałła-1^SG^XR
       I am going (on a trip).

---

[38]The reverse (stative as active) has not been observed.

Some Relevant Features of Koasati Grammar

(34) *canakałła*
  ca-nakałła
  1ˆSGˆDOˆSTAT-*nakałła*
  I am lost (e.g., on a trip or in woods).

(35) *stincaaka amnakałła*
  stincaaka am-nakałła
  pencil   1ˆSGˆIOˆSTAT-*nakałła*
  I lost the pencil (lit: the pencil is lost to me).

The semantics of a switch from active to stative and vice versa is illustrated in examples (36)–(38).

(36) *sobayli-li*
  know-1ˆSGˆXR (NOM)
  I know (active verb).

(37) *ca-sobay-ko*
  1ˆSGˆDOˆSTAT-know-NEG (ACC)
  I don't know (stative verb).

(38) *ci-sobay-takko*[39]
  2ˆSGˆDO-know-1ˆSGˆNEGˆXR (NOM)
  I refuse to acknowledge you (active verb).

The forms in (36) and (37) are far more common than that in (38); KNOWING something is perceived to be a volition state, whereas NOT KNOWING is perceived to be a state of weakness and without volition. The form in (38) in which the subject volitionally rejects knowledge (awareness?) of another person is perceived to be amusing or offensive. Kimball (1985:215) offers the following examples in illustration of the semantics of stative verbs.

(39) *no:cilit*
  no:ci-li-to
  sleep-1ˆSGˆXR-PST
  I slept.

---

[39]The suffix *-takko* is a portmanteau morpheme marking person, number, and negation of a nominative argument.

(40) cano:cit
ca-no:ci-to
1^SG^DO-sleep-PST
I fell asleep.

(41) afa:kalit
afa:ka-li-to
laugh-1^SG^XR-PST
I laughed.

(42) caafa:kat
ca-afa:ka-to
1^SG^DO-laugh-PST
I burst out laughing.

The distinction between active and stative cannot be explained in mere lexical terms but is dependent upon pragmatic factors. In a given instance a speaker may choose to switch from active to stative conjugation for subtle reasons. It is important to note these distinctions because SR marking is sensitive to the pragmatic features shown in active and stative verbs.

The above discussion and glossing strategies adopted in this work are summarized in (43). SR marking can be affected in the environment of stative verbs.

(43) Nomenclature for subject cross-reference in stative verbs

By sets	By case	Abbreviation in glosses	Meaning
I	nominative	(pers. and no.)XR	cross reference
II	accusative	(pers. and no.)DO^STAT	direct object of stative
III	dative	(pers. and no.)IO^STAT	indirect object of stative

3.2.5. Koasati verbal chains. Another feature of Koasati which impacts ±CONT marking is its long VERBAL CHAINS. As Longacre (1985a:250, 264) notes, there is a major typological distinction between co-ranking languages and chaining languages. Examples of uninterrupted chains of twenty or more verbs can be shown in Koasati, and the nature of these chains has great implications for how SR and other features of the grammar work.

The chain and the grammatical hierarchy. Longacre (1983b:43) postulates the existence of a grammatical hierarchy with eight levels as displayed in (44).

(44)   Grammatical hierarchy   Koasati hierarchy

       discourse
       paragraph ⎫
       sentence   ⎪   Area affected
       clause   ⎬   by the
       phrase   ⎪   Koasati
       word   ⎭   chain
       stem
       morpheme

A full discussion of this theoretically complex issue is beyond the scope of this work, but it is safe to observe that in Koasati some of the otherwise distinct levels of the hierarchy are washed out;[40] I have indicated in (44) the areas where distinct levels of the hierarchy are not clearly evident in Koasati. In particular the concepts of both phrase and clause are not highly meaningful for Koasati. Adjectives and adverbs, being verbs, string together to make sequences of verbs and these are sometimes best viewed as just a CHAIN.

This is not to imply that the concept of the chain replaces that of sentence; Longacre (1985a:265) challenges the "fallacious assumption... that such a chain is necessarily a sentence." In Koasati, chains can be linked together to form sentences. On the other hand sentences are sometimes chained together to make paragraphs; all of this can take place with or without use of conjunctions. Longacre (1985a:283) observes that:

> It is a shock to realize... that in some languages, both in New Guinea and South America, we sometimes find chaining carried to such (by our standards) excessive lengths that the chain is plausibly neither a sentence nor a paragraph—unless we consider that the body of a discourse consists of but one sentence or one paragraph.

Some texts (especially those by elderly, articulate speakers delivering monologue narratives) consist of quite lengthy chains which are difficult to break up into sentences without disregarding ±CONT marking linking one section to the next.[41] But of greatest import for the study of SR is the impact of the chain on clause types.

---

[40]Hwang has drawn my attention to Longacre 1983b:295–302 where Longacre points out that all levels of his hierarchy do not occur in many languages.

[41]Burnham (p.c.) has made the same observation.

The chain and clause types. Consider the matter of adjectival clauses about which Kimball (1985:446) states:

> Unlike many other languages of the world, which have special constructions and vocabulary to handle relative clauses, Koasati does not have any distinguishing features that mark certain clauses as being relative.

Similarly, Davis and Hardy (1986) state that "Alabama has no single construction which can be designated as a relative clause." There are several ways in which functional equivalents of relative clauses are encoded including CHAIN EMBEDDING, which I define and discuss in the next section.

Chain embedding. Both (45) and (46) are grammatical, but the form in (46) is expanded to clarify the meaning intended. Parentheses in (45) indicate the location at which the relative clause equivalent was added.

(45) Laura: Rebecca stoklok palkī (...)
     Laura-: Rebecca st-toklo-k palki-˜
     Laura-SER Rebecca INST-be^two-K train

     mathi:caahik aɫacin ...
     mat-hi:ca-aahi-k aɫa-ci-n
     VIA-see-INTN-K go-3^PL^XR-N
     Laura and Rebecca went to see the train (...)

(46) Laura: Rebecca stoklok palki(k ohɫopotli:fooko)-n
     Laura: Rebecca st-toklo-k palki-k oh-ɫopotli-:fooka-n
     Laura: Rebecca INST-be^two-K train-K TRNSL-pass^by-OFFLIN-N

     mathi:caahik aɫacin
     mat-hi:ca-aahi-k aɫa-ci-n
     VIA-see-INTN-K go-3^PL^XR-N
     Laura and Rebecca went to see the train (which was going by).

In (45) nasalization occurs on the word *palki** to indicate its role in this sentence; we can here refer to this as object marking. In (46) the word *ohɫopotli:fooka** is added to clarify that the train the girls went to see was 'passing by'. Note that the surface structure marking on the word *palki** has changed from -˜ to -k. This does not imply that the role of the word *palki** has changed in the sentence; rather the span -k *ohɫopotli:fooka** has

Some Relevant Features of Koasati Grammar 35

been embedded between *palki** and its former marking (-˜). In the process the displaced -˜ has been transformed to an *-n* (which I view as a nonsignificant change).[42] The *-k* added to *palki** relates the word to *ohłopotli:fooka** as subject.

There is no particular morphological device marking this as a relative clause. It is the combination of the verbal chain, the ±CONT marking, embedding, word order, and the semantics of the words involved which indicates the status of each constituent. The structure of the chain can be seen in the following table, an abstraction of (46).

(47) Embedding structure of an RC equivalent

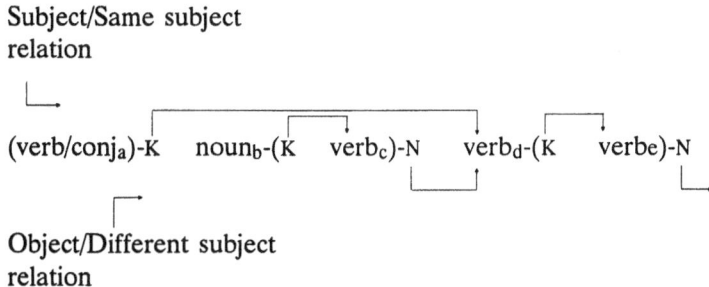

Aside from semantic cues of the words themselves, the Koasati listener disambiguates this string of words in something like the following fashion:

> Verb/conjunction$_a$ with *-k* joins and marks the first two proper nouns as the first subject of the sentence. Noun$_b$ is a second subject, in fact of verb$_c$. Since verb$_d$ is transitive, and verb$_c$ is marked with *-n*, the unit [noun$_b$-k verb$_c$]-*n* serves as an object of verb$_d$, but, since verb$_e$ is marked with *-n*, something new or different will follow, and so forth...

Thompson and Longacre (1985a:172) distinguish three types of subordinate clause: complement, adverbial, and relative. Like the relative clause

---

[42]This illustrates the point made in chapter one that *-n* and -˜ are sometimes interchangeable.

type, the other two formal clause types do not have a distinct formal existence in Koasati. Rather all three are functionally expressed by the Koasati chain.[43]

Embedding as canonical SR. Embedding occurs regularly and frequently in a straightforward manner. Recognizing this phenomenon enables one to explain many cases of SR marking which would otherwise appear exceptional.

(48) okhica tiwaplok cokhalihkok komnałi:kaayon
okhica tiwapli-o-k cokhali*:ka-h-k kom-nałi:ka-ya-o-n
door open-O-K enter-H-K 1^PL^IO-speak-FRUS-O-N

    naason ka:hā kosobaykok maamoosin ...
    naasi-o-n ka:ha-˜ ko-sobayli-ko-k maamoosi-n
    thing-O-N say-˜ 1^PL^DO^STAT-know-3^NEG-K CONJ-N
Opening the door and coming in he tried to speak to us (but) what he said we did not understand and so ...

The salient data in (48) is reproduced below in hybrid form.

(49) to^us^he^try^to^speak-N (what he^said)-˜ we^not^understand-K

From a strictly linear perspective, the verb 'speak' is marked with -*n* with regard to 'said', even though they have the same subject. This is not exceptional marking, but rather an instance of chain embedding. The phrase 'what he said' is a Koasati equivalent of a noun phrase and is a unit functioning as the object of the word 'we did not understand'. Hence the -*n* on the first verb 'speak' is marked with regard to the third verb 'understand' and the -˜ on the second verb 'said' is likewise marked with regard to the third verb. This is illustrated in (50).

---

[43]In free texts there are a plethora of forms that function as relative clauses. I have noted the following: (1) those with -*fooka*, like the one cited in examples (45)-(46); (2) those with the SR marker -*p*; (3) those with the locative *fa*; (4) postposed clauses; (5) those with the third person pronoun *ma**; and (6) others. Finally, somewhat subverting what I have said, there are chain types with the interrogative pronoun *naasi** as well as types with tone changes and addition of verbal suffixes which look like separate relative clause types. These relative clause equivalents occur more frequently in elicitation than in natural discourse. Kimball 1985:448 makes the general comment that "in discourse relative clause equivalents are not common." If, however, we take a loose functional approach to defining relative clause equivalents, including the kinds mentioned in this note, they are seen to be fairly common.

Some Relevant Features of Koasati Grammar

(50) Chain embedding

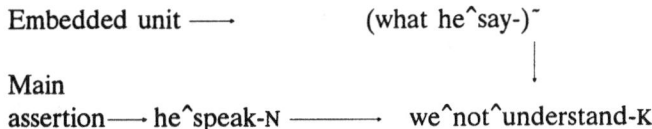

Here the SR marking is seen to be nonexceptional when interpreted in terms of chaining and embedding. In the next examples, the form in (52) contains an embedded relative clause equivalent not found in (51). The patterns of ±CONT marking are similar to those above.

(51) Kathyk   tabahka   i:paahik   bannamp
      Kathy-k   tabahka-ˉ i:paahi-k banna-mpa
      Kathy-K   bread-ˉ   eat-K   want-HRSY
      Kathy wants to eat the bread.

(52) Kathyk   Marianka   tabahka   libatli:kon   i:paahik   bannamp
      Kathy-k   (Marian   tabahka   libatli-:ka-o)-n   i:paahi-k   banna-mpa
      Kathy$_i$-K (Marian$_j$ bread   cook$_j$-TNS-O)-N eat$_i$-K   want$_i$-HRSY
      Kathy wants to eat the bread (which Marian made some time ago).

In (52), the -k marking on *Kathy* does not apply to the immediately following verb *(libatli)* but rather to *i:paahik bannamp*. The clause *(Marianka tabahka libatli:ka*)* is embedded and does not figure in SR marking in the way that verbs in the main chain do: the *-n* on the clause relates not to subject switch but marks the clause as object of the verb *i:pa*. In (51) *tabahka** was the object of *ipa* and was marked with -ˉ; in (52) the whole clause is object and is marked with *-n*. I am uncertain about the missing subject marking on *Marian* since this is usually present.

In the next examples the embedded unit is marked with *-k* and illustrates another kind of embedding.

(53) aatosik   cayahɬ
      aatosi(...)k cayahɬ
      child   walk

(54) aatosi(imkat   ispa:sayo)k⁴⁴   cayahɬ
      aatosi im-ka-t   is-i:pa-:saya-o-k   cayahli-∅
      child   3^IO-give-CONN 2^SG^XR-eat-TNS-O-K walk-3^XR
      The child (whom you just fed) is walking.

Koasati is SOV and usually marks the first subject with *-k*. The *-k* occurring on *ispa:saya** in (54) is the missing subject marking for *aatosi**. In the whole context of the sentence, it is seen that the MATRIX clause is *aatosi-(...)-k cayahɬ* and the EMBEDDED clause is *imkat ispa:saya**, which belongs to the noun phrase constituting the subject and is hence included within the *-k* marking.

This theory works well here but there are troubling examples:

(55) Marianka-k (tabahka ibisnaalo-k libatli:sayo)-k i:paahik bannamp
      Marian-K   (bread   be^self-K   cook-TNS)-?? to^eat   want
      Marian wants to eat (the bread which she herself just made).

Here *-k* (subject) marking occurs on *Marian* as well as on the object clause (which I have parenthesized). By the above reasoning, the third *-k* should have been an *-n*. The resolution of this inconsistency may be that there is a conflict between subject marking and object marking, i.e., the verb *libatli* is SS *(-k)* to the following verb *banna*, but the clause in which *libatli* occurs is also an object *(-n)* to *banna*. Thus the *-k* marking wins out in this conflict.

Another approach is to consider the above from the perspective of ±CONT, rather than from the perspective of subject and object since object is not always fruitful in Koasati. The condition of +CONT between the verbs present ('cook' and 'eat') wins out over other coding needs and hence *-k* is used.

There is evidence that Koasati gives a kind of priority to *-k* marking. In §1.3 of chapter one, I noted that *-k* occurs about twice as frequently as any other SR marker. Munro and Gordon (1982:100, 105) observe that Choctaw prefers certain kinds of SR marking, and it has been noted that some SR languages prefer SS marking. As to why this might be the case, Givón (1984:249) states that:

> At the moment of producing a new proposition ... the ratio of *new information* within that proposition to *old information* in the

---

[44]Literally this is 'to^him^you^give-CONN you^just^eat' but the meaning is 'you just gave him to eat', i.e., 'you just fed him'.

Some Relevant Features of Koasati Grammar   39

discourse *background/context* required for the successful interpretation... of the proposition, is very large.

But it is primarily SAMENESS or OLDNESS that the -*k* is marking (which is the thesis of the next chapter). Thus Givón's observation would predict that -*k* would occur more frequently and would be easier to process.

This overview of Koasati grammar is helpful in understanding the framework in which the Koasati SR markers occur. In the next chapter I explore the underlying functions of -*k* and -*n*.

4
Koasati Continuity Marking

This chapter presents the main argument of this work. It presupposes and builds upon what has been said in the three prior chapters, and in some regards chapter five serves as a further illustration and confirmation of the basic contention of the present chapter. In §4.1 I attempt to demonstrate that the case marking function of -*k* and -*n* on nouns is secondary and that the primary function is to mark INFORMATION TYPE. I then show in §4.2 that the SR function of -*k* and -*n* on verbs is likewise secondary and that the primary function is to mark ±CONT. In §4.3 the two explanations relative to nouns and verbs are united as ±CONT. In §4.4 I make suggestions for further research and observations about the typological implications of this study.

4.1 -*k* and -*n* on nouns: Markers of information type

As with the Muskogean cognates, the usual interpretation of Koasati -*k* and -*n* on nouns is to identify them as case markers. The most fundamental case relations are those of subject and object, whereby subjects are related to the associated verb in a particular way, and likewise objects relate to the verb in a (different) particular way. Linguists have difficulty defining in a universal sense what these particular ways are, but the usefulness of these two notions, and that of case in many languages of the world, is beyond debate. First impressions of Koasati lend credence to a case analysis, but in sustained exposure to data it proves inadequate. In this chapter I argue that the grammatical function of -*k* and -*n* can be described without final reference to subject and object.

The parts of speech distinction between nouns and verbs is intuitively useful in Indo-European languages. For instance, Evans and Evans offer a popular description of the work of an (English) grammarian: "A grammarian groups words that behave similarly into classes and then draws up rules stating how each class of words behaves." As argued in chapter three, this is not the situation which obtains in Koasati. Nouns and verbs are similar formally and functionally. Some sentences just look like strings (chains) of verbs. But why call them 'verbs'... why not just 'words'?

If these reflections are valid, then the very idea of case in Koasati is theoretically unlikely: if nouns and verbs are treated alike then it is not likely that nouns will receive marking to relate them to verbs. Thus we are led to ask just what the morphemes -*k* and -*n* on nouns do encode if they do not say something about a relationship with an associated verb.

Regarding nominal marking in Alabama, Davis and Hardy (1988) have reached conclusions similar to those set forth in this work, stating (284, cf. 289) that the interpretation of case marking is "difficult to maintain." They argue that the fundamental semantics of Alabama -*t*, -*k*, and -*n* are best described on a cline of centrality to peripherality to the proposition, with -*t* being most central, -*n* most peripheral, and -*k* between the two.

The Koasati markers show a great deal of similarity both morphologically and semantically to those of Alabama, and the same three morphemes, -*t*, -*k*, and -*n*, are, relative to one another, on the same cline. However, the semantics of the markers bears closer affinity with Oklahoma Seminole Creek, another Muskogean language, as described by Schuetze-Coburn (1987:146), who states "that all instances of 'anomalous' -*t* and -*n* marking on nominals... function to manage the flow of information in texts." This feature of Koasati -*n* is illustrated in the next examples.

4.1.1. New information marked by -*n* in object slot. In the discourse from which example (56) is taken, the word *Bible* had not yet been introduced; it is marked in two different ways as being NEW INFORMATION. The first way is with the suffix -*o*-;[45] the second is with the marker in

---

[45]The morpheme -*o*- displaces word final -*a*. In this work the morpheme -*o*- is left unglossed and largely undiscussed. Nonetheless, it is relevant to the matter of new versus old information; Jones 1986:306 discusses "the semantics of -*o*- in Coushatta" giving instances in which it indicates new information. He argues further (308) that "while -*o*- occurs with new information, not all new information is marked with -*o*-" and concludes that the term "differentiation" best describes the semantics of the morpheme. In this work I restrict discussion to the concept of new information.

question, -n. Note that in the second occurrence, seen in the third line, the argument *Bible* is marked with -˜; this is a reduction of the semantics of -n. This pattern repeats itself with regularity in free narrative texts. In actual speech, nasalization is not always produced or is produced only when the sentence would be ambiguous in its absence. Thus there are two stages of reduction of the morpheme -n on nouns: to nasalization or to zero.

(56) *Biblekon lonhit komsuitcasekafã aɬit*
Bible-o-n lonhi-t kom-suitcase-fã aɬi-t
Bible-O-N be^secret-CONN 1^PL^IO-suitcase-LOC load-CONN

anoslok stanɬi:yak. Romaniakafã Biblekã
ano:li^PL-o-k st-aɬi:ya^DU-k Romania-fã Bible-˜
finish-O-K INST-we^2^go-K Romania-LOC Bible-˜

hobannkot ohaki:lohci
ho-banna-ko-t ho-aki:lo-hci
3^PL-want-3^NEG-CONN 3^PL-not^permit-ASP
We went to Romania with Bibles hidden in our suitcases. In Romania they do not permit Bibles.

In (57), the opening line of a story about a business trip to Canada, -n again marks new information, occurring this time on the locative marker *fa**. Note that the -n-marking is again reduced to nasalization in the second occurrence, encoding the movement from new to old information; -n, as a marker of newness, encodes information as new or –CONT.

(57) *acaffaakan Vancouver, Canadakafon mathokotohnon*
acaffaakan Vancouver, Canada-fa-o-n mathokotohnon
once Vancouver, Canada-LOC-O-N they^sent^us

... *Canadafã*
... *Canada-fa-˜*
... Canada-LOC-˜
Once we were sent to Canada ... there in Canada ...

In the above examples -n correlates with information type, and all the examples have occurred on arguments in oblique cases. In §4.1.2 I demonstrate that -n sometimes occurs on subjects specifically because they are new information; this allows us to further disassociate the marker from the concept of case. Then in §4.1.3 I demonstrate that, *mutatis mutandis*, the same thing occurs with the marker *-k:* it occurs on obliques under certain (rare) circumstances in which subject marking conflicts with ±CONT marking.

4.1.2. New information marked by *-n* in subject slot. In example (58), *-n* marks an argument which is the surface structure subject of a stative verb and which is statistically more likely to be associated with *-k*.

(58)   *mafã   kayakkon   amnaahohcoolik*
       ma-fã   kayak-o-n   am-naaho-∅-hci-ooli-k
       there-LOC kayak-O-N   1^SG^IO^STAT-exist-3^XR-ASP-ASP-K
       There I used to have a kayak (lit. to^me-existed).

The word 'kayak' is new information, and the author has chosen to encode this with *-n*. The English gloss suggests that first singular is the subject of this sentence, but the word 'kayak' is the morphosyntactic subject; literally it reads, 'there a kayak existed to me'. The verb in this example is stative, and subject assignment in such verbs is open to some debate. A complete discussion[46] of this subject would go beyond the confines of this work, but (59) illustrates the marking of arguments which occurs more frequently with the verb *naaho*. Note that in this example there are three third-person plural arguments; I have added subscripts to help trace these arguments.

(59)   *mafap   Christiankaha-∅   yaamik   Bibleskak*
       ma-fa-p   Christian-PL-∅   yaami-k   Bibles-k
       there-LOC-P   Christians   be^like-K   Bibles-K

       imnaahaahī   *hobannkohci*
       im-naaho-∅-aahi-ˉ   *ho-banna-ko-hci*
       3^IO^STAT-exist-3^XR-INTN-ˉ   3^PL-want-3^NEG-ASP
       There they (the rulers) don't want Christians (or anyone else) to have Bibles (lit. there Christians$_a$ (and^those^like^them) Bibles$_b$-k to^them$_a$^they$_b$^exist they$_c$^don't^want).

The relevant portions of this sentence are:

---

[46]Compare Munro and Gordon (1982) who discuss subject assignment in Choctaw and the problem of stative verbs. Their analysis does not invariably hold true for Koasati.

(60) ... *Christiankaha-∅*   *Bibleskak*   *imnaahaahī* ...
       Christian-PL-∅   *Bibles-k*   *im-naaho-∅-aahi-˜*
       Christians   Bibles-K   3ˆIOˆSTAT-exist-3ˆXR-INTN-˜

The word *Christian* is marked with ∅ but is cross-referenced on the verb by -*im* (3ˆIOˆSTAT); in turn the word *Bibles* is marked with -*k* but cross-referenced by -∅ (3ˆXR). The zero cross-reference marking on *naaho* is what cross-references the third-person surface-structure subject in highly transitive, active verbs. Since it here cross-references *Bibles*, we see that *Bibles* is the surface-structure subject, and indeed the word itself is marked by -*k* (associated with subject case). This is statistically the most common marking, although ∅ and -˜ do also occur. In contrast, -*n* marking is rare, and in my data its occurrence is conditioned by information type, as in example (58).

As stated, *naaho* is a stative verb, and stative verbs have skewed subject marking. What of the occasion when the subject of an active verb is new information? In such cases -*k* normally is used, even when it marks an argument which is new information, and other devices[47] are used to signal the information flow. This occurrence of new information with -*k* constitutes a challenge to my thesis. In the context of active verbs, -*k* marking has a strong correlation to subject case marking so that its function can almost be explained on the level of syntax. Nonetheless, I have found examples of -*n* marking a new information argument which is associated with the subject of an active verb; a first example is given in (61).

(61) *1972kakitton*   *amoklon*   *stoliklok*
      1972-kitton   *am-okla-o-n*   *st-to*klo-li-k*
      1972-longˆago   1ˆSGˆIO-friend-O-N INST-beˆtwo-1ˆPLˆXR-K

      Germanykafon   *ontok*   *aliswahcoolik*
      Germany-fa-o-n *o:ta-o-k*   *a*swa-li-hci-ooli-k*
      Germany-LOC-O-N weˆarrive-O-K   liveˆDU-1ˆPLˆXR-ASP-ASP-K
      A long time ago in 1972 my friend and I went to Germany and lived there.

This is the opening line of a story, and the friend is put on stage with -*n*, the new information marker. Subsequently in this discourse the same

---

[47]There are a number of devices employed, and a full discussion of this subject is beyond the scope of this work, though I will note two strategies. (1) In footnote 45 above I mentioned the new information marker -*o*- which can be used in conjunction with -*k*: *aatok aati-o-k* (person-NI-SJ) and *aatik aati-∅-k* (person-OI-SJ). (2) There are also cleft constructions with the auxiliary verb *ommi* with a -*k* suffix.

two arguments appear as *amokla* (+∅) *stoliklo-k* with the same gloss: 'my friend and I'. Arguments followed by conjunctive verbs such as *toklo* 'the two of them' are almost always left unmarked (see example (62) below). That *okla* is new information conditions this occurrence of *-n* on the syntactic subject of a verb.

(62) *ihoocakon   anoo-∅   Mary-∅   komatlowista-∅   kaamit*
     awhile^ago   1^SG^PRO   Mary   our-kids   be^all-PST

   yomahhlin   hinifa
   we^went   on^road
   Awhile back Mary, our kids, and I were driving down the road.

The arguments *anoo, Mary*, and *atlowista* are all unmarked and the final subject marking *-t*[48] on *kaami** 'be all' is understood to apply to all the preceding nouns.

The next example illustrates the tension in Koasati between ±CONT marking and case marking. Examples (63) and (64) alternate opening lines of a narrative and are grammatical and equivalent ways of encoding the new information.

(63) *acaffaakan   amoklon   Jimkon*
     acaffaakan   am-okla-o-n   Jim-o-n
     once   1^SG^IO-friend-O-N Jim-O-N

   stałi:yalik   imokwayhillaho
   st-ałi:ya-li-k   imokwayli-hili-laho[49]
   INST-go-1^SG^XR-K   fish-1^PL^XR-IRR
   Once I went with my friend, Jim—we went fishing.

(64) *acaffaak   stałi:yalik   amoklon   Jimkon*
     acaffaakan st-ałi:ya-li-k   am-okla-n   Jim-o-n
     once   INST-go-1^SG^XR-K   1^SG^IO-friend-N Jim-O-N

---

[48]*-t* marking occurs as subject marking, rather than the more common *-k*, under circumstances not fully understood. *-t* commonly occurs as subject marking on numbers and words like *kaami**. In the cognate languages Choctaw and Alabama, *-t* is the common marker of subject.

[49]The use of the irrealis (future 1) suffix in this example is not understood.

Koasati Continuity Marking

  holcifok łaton imokwayhillaho
  holcifo-k łato-n imokwayli-hili-laho
  be^name-K fish-N fish-1^PL^XR-IRR
Once I went with someone—my friend is named Jim—we went fishing.

An idea of the function of the prefix *st-* is essential for understanding these examples. Hardy and Davis state that the Alabama prefix *ist-*, which occurs with very similar semantics, marks an "implied participant" or a "peripheral-to-proposition participant" (1989:32). Elsewhere they (1988:213) state:

> ... the presence of the *ist-* prefix ... permits the addition of a second PARTICIPANT ... to what would otherwise be a single-PARTICIPANT stative EVENT.

Similarly the Koasati *st-* prefix raises the valency of a verb. Its use is not restricted to verb type or to just participants. Its presence on a verb sometimes has an effect of indicating that something else is involved or acted upon without specifying what that other thing might be as shown in (65).

(65) *ałi:yal*   'I am going'
   stałi:yal   'I am going with someone or
          (carrying) something' [comitative]
   ałłal   'I am going'
   stałłal   'I am going in or by means of something'
          (car?, bike?) [instrumental]

In (63) the new information argument 'my friend Jim' is introduced in a non-nominative slot, which is cross-linguistically the grammatical location at which new information is most likely to occur (see discussion below). But even though it occurs as the object, it is in some sense the subject (main clausal topic, pragmatic peak)[50] of this sentence as can be seen from the +CONT marking: *-k* connects (1) a verb *(stałi:yali*)* in which Jim occurs as morphosyntactic object with (2) a verb *(imokwayhillaho)* in which Jim is included in the morphosyntactic subject set.

In (64) the presentative verb *holcifo* 'he is named, he names' is used with the new information. In both (63) and (64) the author asserts that he and his friend went fishing, but there is an information conflict. In the first

---

[50]The above argument contains an oxymoron (the object is the subject). This hints at the inappropriateness of the concepts of subject and object for describing Koasati.

place, the 'friend' was new information and this is normally marked with -*n*. On the other hand, this 'friend' was also the subject which is normally marked with -*k*. This leads to the kinds of circumlocutions seen here to avoid conflict between the primary function of -*k* and -*n* as markers of information type and their secondary function as markers of case.

4.1.3. Old information marked by -*k* in object slot. The next step is to find -*k* marking on arguments which are oblique.[51] The following example is from a tape-recorded message sent by a group of friends to a lady who was hospitalized in a distant town.

(66) isno-k   poli:katiska-p kosno-k   mat-ko-sob:ayli-˜
       2 SGˆPRO-K youˆpray-P   1ˆPLˆPRO-K DIST-1ˆSGˆDO-remember-DELAY
       as for you if you pray   we/us   remember us
       When/if you pray, remember us.

As stated earlier, personal pronouns are rarely used; in (66) and (67) their presence encodes emphasis. It is clear that the word *kosno* is oblique: the direct object prefix *ko-* cross-references the same argument as *kosno*. Yet *kosno* is marked with -*k*. The purpose of this marking is not understood, and language consultants were unable to offer an explanation. A consideration is that one would normally expect the healthy to pray for the sick; thus the -*k* marking, simply because it is abnormal, connotes an expectancy reversal.[52] The next example is a prayer taken from a tape recorded sermon.

(67) himayap isno-k   am-okcaliya ommik ohyā
       now   2ˆSGˆPRO-k   1ˆSGˆIO-life AUX   beˆall-˜
       now   you (OBL!)   my life   CLFT   all of it

       cim-fahli-li-n
       2ˆSGˆIOˆgiveˆup-1ˆSGˆXR-N
       I give to you
       Now it is my life I completely deliver up to you (God).

'God', the second singular argument, is cross-referenced both by the pronoun *isno* and by the prefix *cim*. The -*k* appears to be marking focus or topic or pragmatic peak: it communicates that the prayer has God in

---
[51]Such examples are quite rare. -*k* marking correlates strongly with subject case marking and, frankly, it was with disbelief that I recognized the following examples.
[52]This was also suggested by Longacre (p.c.).

focus rather than human actions. A translation using cleft focus reflects these semantics: 'Now *it is unto you* and it is my life that I completely deliver up'. This interpretation accords with that of Davis and Hardy (1988:285) who report that on Alabama nouns "-*k* communicates a greater degree of purpose, an increased focus ... on the goal to be achieved [than does -*n*]."

4.1.4. Relationship of case and information flow. The following table shows the functions of -*k* and -*n* on nouns.

(68) A new interpretation of -*k* and -*n* on nouns

I	II	III
SR marker	Function is to mark	OI and NI are usually but not always associated with
-*k*	old info, topic	subject case
-*n*	new info	object case

The elements of column II are intrinsically related to the semantics of -*k* and -*n*/-˜; the elements of column III are not directly related to -*k* and -*n*/-˜ but rather to those of column II, and the relationship between column II and column III is only as strong as the tendency for Koasati subjects to be old information and, vice versa, objects to be new information. This tendency is language universal as Givón (1984:256) states:

> Propositions in real discourse context, then, are most commonly informational hybrids, so that some portions of them are *old, presupposed,* or *background* information, presumably serving to anchor them within the coherence structure of discourse ... while other portions are under the scope of asserted new information. Most commonly, the *subject* ('main clausal topic') *tends to be part of the* old information in clauses, while the rest of the clause has a higher likelihood of being new information.

-*k* tends to mark subject and -*n* tends to mark object, but there is no intrinsic relationship.

Thus far I have reinterpreted the role of the ±CONT markers on nouns; in the next section I reinterpret the role of the markers on verbs. The reinterpretation is in line with that just presented and allows us to give more meaning to the term continuity.

4.2 -k and -n on verbs: Markers of ±CONT

The above section on case began with a discussion of the notions of subject and object in Koasati and observed that, if they are not highly relevant to Koasati grammar, then it is not likely that the language would have a complex subject case-marking system. With the same reasoning one might suspect that it is not likely that the language would have a developed means of tracing subject. I begin by investigating an occasion when the markers -k and -n join a verb to the auxiliary verb *ommi* where *ommi* is not marked for person and number.[53] The semantics of -k and -n in combination with this auxiliary provide crucial support for the thesis of this chapter.

4.2.1. Linking -k and -n to *ommi*. Example (69) shows the relative frequencies of five[54] ±CONT markers which occur with *ommi*.

(69)

±CONT marker	Occurrences with *ommi*	Typical form
-k	200+	*hcok om*[55]
-n	20−	*hcon om*
-p	1	*hcop om*
-t	16	*hcot om*
-tik	2	*hcotik om*

In terms of absolute frequency, the phonological pattern... *verb-hcok om*... is heard constantly. Of primary interest is the semantic difference between the *-k om* and the *-n om* combinations; the following presents a minimal pair.

(70) amifa-k wali:kahco-k om
my^dog-K is^running-K AUX
My dog is running, of course, as expected.

---

[53]The word is comparable to English 'to be' and 'to do' and has a host of functions. It also occurs in a different environment and use with person/number marking.

[54]These are all the markers which have been noted to occur with *ommi*.

[55]*ommi* is shortened to *om* in the absence of suffixal marking (Kimball 1985 describes this as DEL "word final vowel deletion").

(71) amifa-k   wali:kahco-n   om
     my^dog-K   is^running-N   AUX
     My dog is running, against expectations.

Here -*k* and -*n* are not tracing subject because the auxiliary *ommi* simply has no subject to trace. Rather, they are marking a kind of ±CONT as suggested by the added glosses. It is impossible to fully gloss such forms out of discourse context, but the general semantics of -*k* and -*n* shine through in this example where -*n* is seen to correlate with −CONT and -*k* with +CONT. In the next example a man had just fallen into a wasp nest and was covered with hundreds of wasps.

(72) *falankalok*   *mantik*   *wali:kalitikap*   *ittihaplit*
     falanka-li-k   mantik   wali:ka-li-tikap   itti-hapli-t
     get^up-1^SG^XR-K   but   run-1^SG^XR-like^mad   RECIP-fight-CONN
     I got up and   ??   I ran like mad   fighting them

    wali:kalitik   *ampartner*   *mok*
    wali:ka-li-tik   am-partner   ma-o-k
    run-1^SG^XR-but   1^SG^IO-partner   3^PRO-O-K
    I ran but   my partner   he

    immankalip   *piila wali:kahcon   ommik   mok*
    im-manka-li-p   piila wali:ka-hci-n   ommi-k   ma-o-k
    3^IO-call^to-1^SG^XR-P(IRR) just run-ASP-2OM   AUX-K   3^PRO-O-K
    though I called to him   just ran away   he RDLOC

I got up (out of the nest) and ran like mad fighting [the wasps] and running but even though I called to my partner that guy just ran away!

About the semantics of the -*n om* combination, a language guide commented, "He was mad." He was angry that his partner did not come to his aid. However, the combination of -*n* and *ommi* does not necessarily imply anger; its meaning in this sentence must be inferred from context and the underlying semantics of -*n*.

In the next two examples the -*n om* combination encodes similar sentiments. In example (73) a child had unsuccessfully attempted to make a whistle according to instructions from his grandfather. He asked his grandfather:

(73) maalohkohcon   talibohlilin   ommit   ooli
     maalo-ko-hci-n   talibo:li-li-n   ommi-t   ooli
     be^right-NEG-ASP-N make-1^SG^XR-2OM   AUX-CONN   TAG
     it is not right   I make [it]   AUX   TAG
     Didn't I make it right?

The child was disappointed; the -n encodes the expectancy reversal of making something that does not work.

The following is from the translation of the Christmas story where Joseph and Mary arrive in Bethlehem and find the inn full:

(74) itinocafak alotkahchotoho-n ommi-to
     the^inn-K be^full-2OM   AUX-PST
     (Unfortunately) the inn was full.

In all of these examples the -n om combination encodes some kind of disappointment, anger, or indignation; the auxiliary verb *ommi* draws out the deeper semantics of -n which are −CONT or some disruption of expectations, hopes, or the like.

The -k om combination occurs quite frequently yet is difficult to gloss.[56] Speakers of the language accept forms with and without the auxiliary verb as equivalent. For instance, in isolation and as a means of describing someone smiling, language consultants state that the two forms in (75) are identical.

(75) afa:kahci   'he is smiling'
     afa:kahcok om   'he is smiling'

The function of the combination of -k and *ommi* is almost certainly rooted in discourse factors, but the following example indicates that it connotes a kind of heightening or emphasis of the verb to which it is attached. A mother addressing her young child standing up precariously in a highchair builds to a crescendo:

(76) cokkol!   'sit down'   first command (no response)
     cokkol!   second command (still no response)
     cokkolok om!   third command with loud voice.
                                   (child sat down!)

---

[56]Kimball usually glosses *ommi* 'be', and Burnham (unpublished ms.) glosses with 'x'. Even harder to gloss are examples in which the *ommi* occurs 'two deep' as in *tamookatik ayyahcot ommok ommitos* 'even though at night he went of course I guess' —I think!

Koasati Continuity Marking

Thus the semantics of -*k* and -*n*, in combination with the auxiliary, support the theory of ±CONT: -*k om* added to a verb emphasizes its semantics (+CONT) and -*n om* marks some kind of disruption (-CONT). Note that it is not the semantics of the auxiliary verb *ommi* which leads to this interpretation; it is the semantics of -*k* and -*n* which are drawn out in combination with *ommi*.

I now turn attention to data in which -*k* and -*n* appear between fully conjugated verbs but do so in ways which are anomalous to traditional SR theory.

4.2.2. Anomalous -*k* and -*n* between verbs. The kinds of examples which would support the theory of ±CONT are those in which (1) the +CONT function of -*k* overrules its SS marking function and (2) the -CONT function of -*n* overrules its DS marking function. In other words, situations in which (1) there is a DS condition between two verbs, but the verbs are marked with -*k* (due to a +CONT situation), or, vice versa, (2) one in which there is a SS condition which is marked with -*n* (due to a -CONT situation). Example (77) is an example of the condition (1).

(77) Notional structure: +CONT and DS marked by -*k*

miita mok	ilma:kat	itcokkahkak
miita ma-o-k	ilma:ka-t	it-cokkahka-k
other 3^PRO-O-K	come^PL-CONN	ILL-enter^PL-K

fayahkok	alotkaahosit	ano:kak
fayahli-ō-ko-k	alotka-aahosi-t	ano:ka-k
quit^PL-3^NEG-+CONT	be^full-very-CONN	be^done-K

roomkasik	coki:boshcooliskan
room-si-k	co*:ba-ki-si-hci-ooli-skan
room-DIM-K	be^big-3^NEG-DIM-ASP-ASP-CAUS

Other people did not stop coming and entering until the room was completely full since it was quite small.

The salient portions of (77) are reproduced in the following hybrid:

(78) clause 1: others coming entering not^stop-K
 clause 2: was^very^filled up (AUX) the^little^room ...

In this example -*k* on *fayahko** links verbs with disjoint subject sets: 'other people' and 'a little room'. Rather than tracing subject, -*k* is encoding a kind of connectedness or +CONT between the two clauses. The nature of this connectedness gives insight into its deeper function. One intuitively sees a causal connection between clause 1 and clause 2, and this connection is encoded but not spelled out by the -*k*. In my free translation I have used the word 'until', but the author's intention may have been to say, 'people came in *and so* the little room got full' or other possible interpretations. Note that the continuity marked is not one of topic or subject but of action.

In examples (77)–(78) the connection between clause 1 and clause 2 is encoded by -*k* as a suffix on a verb; -*k* can also occur as a suffix on a CONJUNCTION between two clauses and have the same effect:

(79) Notional structure: +CONT and DS marked by -*k*

naasi ohya   stimannoslit   stama:kak   ma:mok
naasi ohya   st-im-annosli-t   st-ama:ka-∅-k   ma:mo-k
thing be^all   INST-3^IO-torture-CONN   INST-go^PL-3-K   CONJ-+CONT
all sorts of   do bad things to   they do   so that

mafap   baptizekat   hacca:cip   immayap   schoolkā
ma-fa-p   baptize-t   hacca:li-ci-p   immayap   school-⁻
there-LOC-P   baptize-CONN   stand-2^SG^XR-P   be^more   school-⁻
there   baptized   if you are   to more   school

cokhalicikkohci
cokhali:ka-cikko-hci
go^in-2^SG^NEG^XR-ASP
you will not go

They inflict all kinds of bad things to (torture) people and/so if you are baptized you cannot go to school.

In a hybrid form this is:

(80) clause 1: they do all sorts of bad things *MA:MO-K*
      clause 2: (if you are baptized) you will not go to more school

The clauses before and after *ma:mok* are clearly in a DS condition (third plural to second singular) but are intimately related in content: the clause following *ma:mok* is a specific example of the statement in the clause preceding. The *-k* is not tracing participants but rather marking the +CONT which obtains between the clauses conjoined.

In the next example the reverse condition obtains: SS and −CONT. The *-n* marking contradicts the SS situation but encodes the −CONT condition.

(81)   Notional structure: −CONT and SS marked by *-n*

Noahk piła talibo:lit   staɬi:yatoolimpahco   maamoosin
Noah-k piła talibo:li-t   st-aɬi:ya-toolimpa-hci-o maamoosi-n
Noah-K boat make-CONN INST-go-ASP-ASP-O   CONJ.−CONT
Noah   boat make   he went about   so then

  (piła talibo:lit   staɬi:ya:fookok   ommi:k)
  (piła talibo:li-t   st-aɬi:ya-:fooka-k   ommi-k)
  (boat make-CONN INST-go-OFFLIN-2OM AUX-K)
  (boat make   while he was making   )

Noahk   aatimayba:cit
Noah-k   aatim-ayba:ci-t
Noah-K   HUM^IO-warn-CONN
Noah   people warned

Noah went about making the boat and meantime (while he was making the boat) he warned the people.

We need to recognize, first of all, that the conjunctive word *maamoosi-n* is relating the two verbs, *staɬi:yatoolimpahco* and *aatimayba:cit*. These two verbs contain mainline information, whereas the intervening verb with the suffix *-fooka* is offline (I have added parentheses to set apart the offline clause). This matter is the subject of chapter five and will not be discussed further here. The salient verbs are displayed in the following hybrid example with the ellipsis indicated.

(82)   Noah-K the^boat was^making *maamoosi-n* (...)
       Noah-K the^people^warned

Both verbs in (81)–(82) have Noah as subject yet they are linked with *-n*. It appears that the marking reflects that the activity of constructing the boat and of preaching are unrelated temporally or causally, as suggested in the free translation 'meantime'.

4.3 -*k* and -*n* on nouns and verbs in terms of ±CONT

In §4.1 I showed that the markers -*k* and -*n* cannot properly be analyzed as case markers but rather encode information flow. In the first half of §4.2 I examined a use of the markers -*k* and -*n* which is altogether unrelated to tracing of participants and showed that here it encodes disruption, surprise, or disappointment. In the second half of §4.2 I examined occurrences of -*k* and -*n* which are anomalous to SR theory and showed that these instances could be explained by viewing -*k* and -*n* as markers of various kinds of ±CONT. I now wish to put both these results together in one coherent theory.

There is a crosslinguistic connection between subjects and old information, and, likewise, one relating objects and new information. This was pointed out in the above quote from Givón (1984:256) and is seen again here (1984:206–7):

> The pragmatic principle which controls word-order variation in Ute, one which has been shown to apply similarly elsewhere, may be summarized as:
>
> 36. "More surprising/disruptive/new information precedes more continuous/predictable/old information."

On the other hand, Givón continues, the opposite principle obtains for Mandarin:

> 37. "More indefinite/discontinuous/new information follows more definite/continuous/old information."

Example (83) summarizes the connection between the elements cited by Givón in 36 and 37 above.

(83)   Relationship of -*k* and -*n* to information flow

SR marker	Information type encoded	Markedness
-*k*	continuous, predictable, OI	unmarked
-*n*	surprising, disruptive, NI	marked

Koasati Continuity Marking

Givón points out the universal semantic relationship between NEWNESS and −CONT, and this is what is found with *-n* on nouns (newness) and verbs (discontinuity). *-k*, on the other hand, is the unmarked case (in the Praguian sense), whether it be on nouns or verbs, where the general flow of information and semantics is allowed to go on uninterrupted.

Another way to conceive of *-k* marking is that it marks inertia: when a Koasati speaker produces a word with a *-k* he does so to signal that the general direction, momentum, or "conversational implicature" (Watkins 1987:320) is maintained in what follows.

The notions marked by the ±CONT system are diverse. Givón (1983b:53–4) sheds light on this issue.

There are three major levels of continuity in discourse:

(a) Thematic continuity
(b) *Action* continuity
(c) Participants or *topics* [sic] continuity.

He states that levels (b) and (c)

are intimately involved in defining both the structure of the thematic paragraph and the syntax of sentences/clauses... Action continuity is the domain of chaining verbs/predications one after another within the thematic paragraph in a way that *coheres* or *makes temporal or causal sense*... While action continuity is often inseparable in live discourse from participant/topic continuity, I will have little to say about it here.(6)

The number six refers to a footnote which I would also like to cite:

In live discourse, action continuity and topic continuity most often go hand in hand... *Occasionally, the very same syntactic device is used to code either* discontinuity in a language.

Koasati is an example of a language which uses the "very same syntactic device" to mark different levels of continuity. In fact it is difficult to analyze them separately. I am now able to construct the table in (84) which describes all the functions of *-k* and *-n/-˜*.

I would postulate that further research will show that the interrelationships between the morphemes *-t*, *-k*, *-˜*, and *-n* as seen in (85) hold true. This table says that *-t* is the marker used to encode the highest +CONT condition and -*n* for the highest −CONT condition. The semantics of -*k* and -˜ are between those of -*t* and -*n*. This cline resembles those found in Davis and Hardy (1988:290–94) for Alabama -*t*, -*k*, and -*n*.

(84)   -*k* and -*n* in Koasati

	On Nouns		On Verbs	
Marker	Information type	Usual grammatical role	Discourse/Pragmatic function	Usual SR role
-*k*	+CONT, old, predictable	subject	+CONT, inertia	SS
-*n*	−CONT, new	oblique	−CONT, unexpected, surprise	DS

(85)   Semantic relationships of ±CONT markers

+CONT			−CONT
inertia			disruption
stability			instability
-*t*	-*k*	-˜	-*n*

4.4 Conclusion

The function of the markers -*k* and -*n*/-˜ has been described within one overarching theory of continuity. In practice one may sometimes still want to gloss them in terms of switch referencing and case marking as I have done in this work; this is especially true of the role of -*k* on nouns which almost invariably marks subject case. But properly speaking -*k* and -*n* on verbs ought not to be designated as markers of switch reference but rather continuity. Likewise the markers on nouns ought not to be described as markers of case but continuity.

This new perspective on the function of the markers should enable a better understanding of the grammar of Koasati. It may also have implications for typological understanding of the concept of continuity, as Koasati is an example of a language in which a broad concept of continuity is found.

In chapter one, §1.2.3, and footnote 16 I discussed the larger storehouse of markers of which -*k* and -*n* are a part. Further study of the members of this list, clearly not SR markers, promises to shed further insight into the Koasati ±CONT marking system.

5
Spectrum, -*Fooka*, and Switch Reference

In the preceding chapter I argued that Koasati exceptional marking "necessitates an account not limited to a syntactic switch-reference analysis."[57] The marking system is best understood as a ±CONT marking system which is influenced by discourse-pragmatic factors such as (nominal) information type, inertia, etc. In this chapter I attempt to show that ±CONT marking is influenced by another discourse feature, SPECTRUM, marked by the verbal suffix -*fooka*. Thus this chapter has two goals: first I further explore the ±CONT marking system of Koasati, and second contribute to an understanding of Koasati discourse.

The chapter is organized as follows. Section §5.1 serves as a lemma, introducing the notion of spectrum, a term used by Longacre (1981) to describe PROMINENCE found in discourse, and then making observations about -*fooka*. Following this I show how -*fooka* functions to break Koasati discourse into a spectrum. In §5.3 the interaction of -*fooka* with SR and ±CONT marking is demonstrated. I then address some possible concerns with some reflections and counter-examples in §5.4 and §5.5. In conclusion I make observations about this study and suggestions for further work.

5.1 The concept of spectrum and -*fooka*

5.1.1. The concept of spectrum. The terms SPECTRUM and PROFILE were introduced by Longacre to describe the texture of discourse (1981:337):

---

[57]Borrowing the wording chosen by Hardy and Davis 1988:221 for their conclusion reached with similar data in Alabama.

> Both... have to do with the complementary concerns of cohesion and prominence in discourse structure; that spectrum has to do largely with continuing strands of information which at once unite a discourse and distinguish hierarchically the types of information within it...

This chapter is concerned with the concept of spectrum which is taken metaphorically from optics; Longacre (1981:340) says that:

> Just as a spectographic analysis of white light separates out various hues... so the analysis of a narrative text reveals a cline of information which ranges from the most dynamic elements of the story to the most static (depictive) elements...

Longacre (1989) uses the term RANK SCHEME to refer to spectrum and presents a table which illustrates the makeup of this cline and the general thrust of the concept of spectrum. This table is reproduced in (86) in a shortened and adapted form.

(86) English spectrum/rank scheme (Longacre 1989:416)

Band 1 Storyline	Past action Past cognitive events	
Band 2 Background	Past progressive background activities	
Band 3 Flashback	Pluperfects (Events out of sequence)	
Band 4 Setting	Stative verbs 'Be'/'have' verbs	
Band 5 Irrealis	Negatives Modals	
Band 6 Evaluation	Past tense (cf. setting)	
Band 7 Cohesive band (verbs in preposed/ postposed adverbial clauses)	Repetitive Back reference	

A variety of nomenclature has been employed to describe the divisions of discourse texture, sometimes leaving uncertainty about the nature of the cuts, whether they were taken at the same angle, whether they were taken down the middle or to one side, etc. Some of the terminology found is displayed in (87).

(87) Terminology for the binary division of the spectrum

Half A	Half B	Source
Event	Non-event	Grimes[58]
Events	Background	Jones and Jones[59]
Backbone or foreground	Background	Jones and Jones[59] and Longacre[60]
Foreground	Background	Hopper[61]
Event line	Supportive material	Longacre[62]
Mainline	Subsidiary, ancillary material	Longacre[62]
Storyline	Off line	Longacre[62]
	Other material	Longacre[62]
Time line		Others
Skeleton		

This terminology reflects a general binary perspective, but Longacre (p.c.) opposes the view that spectrum is limited to a binary form (hence the term SPECTRUM). He does, however, make a categorical distinction between MAINLINE and all other levels of discourse; this is the point of Hypothesis I in his 1989 article "Two hypotheses regarding text generation and analysis":

> Hypothesis I: It is assumed here that for any language each type of text has a main line of development and contains other materials which can be conceived of as encoding progressive degrees of departure from the main line. (414)

---

[58]Grimes 1975. Chapter three of this book is entitled "Events and participants in discourse" and chapter four is "Non-events in discourse," whereby non-events consist of setting, background, evaluations, and collateral.

[59]Jones and Jones 1979. In part one, the authors introduce their subject and discuss different kinds of nomenclature used. The main distinction used by Jones and Jones is that between events and background.

[60]Longacre 1976.

[61]Hopper 1979.

[62]These are some of the terms used by Longacre in articles since 1980. See especially 1981, 1983b:14, and 1989.

The mainline constitutes the "main structural feature of the story" (1989:414); thus discourse consists broadly of mainline and nonmainline elements. The mainline consists mainly of events, and from these events the discourse is derived by progressive additions of nonmainline material or demotion of mainline.

That the distinction is not only binary is seen in that the mainline itself can in some languages be subdivided (over against other levels, such as background information) as Longacre (1989:421, 424–5) demonstrates of Totonac, Aguacatec, and Kickapoo. In these languages the main action verbs in the language are divided morphosyntactically into mainline and secondary mainline.

The verbal suffix *-fooka* is one means used to give Koasati discourse a spectrum; the suffix is specifically a DEMOTING tool used to lower verbs away from the mainline. This is not to say that the marker occurs only on mainline verbs; it occurs on a variety of verbs which encode a variety of information types. But *-fooka* lowers verbs in dynamicity and punctiliarness or it encodes that their sequentiality has in some way been altered.[63] If *-fooka* occurs on what was a mainline verb, it lowers it off the mainline; if *-fooka* occurs on, say, a verb marking background information, it further demotes that verb, perhaps creating a category of routine background information. In this work I limit discussion to a coarse-grain perspective and refer to *-fooka*-marked verbs as OFFLINE verbs in contradistinction to MAINLINE verbs.

It is insightful to compare the function of Koasati *-fooka* with the spectrum of English as given in (86). I find that *-fooka*-marked verbs encode background information (Band 2), flashback information (Band 3), setting (Band 4), and, frequently, cohesion/back-reference (Band 7).

5.1.2. Morphology and semantics of *-fooka*.

Morphology. Verbs on which *-fooka* occur tend to have a reduced amount of morphological marking,[64] and most commonly have only certain prefixes, subject and object inflection, and ±CONT marking. Occasionally *-fooka*-marked verbs are also conjugated for tense and a limited number of adverbial suffixes as illustrated in the next few examples.

---

[63]Dynamicity, punctiliarness, and sequentiality are essential features of mainline verbs, as is pointed out by Hopper 1979:215–6, Hopper and Thompson 1980, and Longacre 1989. To further discuss this matter is beyond the scope of this work.

[64]Noted also by Kimball 1985:182–3. Kimball states that the suffix never occurs with tense marking, but I have found instances of same.

(88) Rebecca Laura stoklook   mathi:caahi:fookon
     Rebecca Laura st-toklo-k   mat-hi:ca-aahi-:fooka-n
     Rebecca Laura INST-be^two-K DIST-see-INTN-OFFLIN-N
     Rebecca Laura both   (intending to) see over there

    Gregka mok   mathicaahik   bannok ...
    Greg   mo-k   mat-hi:ca-aahi-k   banna-o-k
    Greg   3^PRO-K DIST-see-INTN-K   want-O-K
    Greg   also   to go see afar   wanted

Laura and Rebecca had gone to look, and Greg also wanted to go look.

Here *-fooka* occurs with the suffix *-aahi* which encodes the irrealis notions of future tense and purpose. In the original discourse, it is the actions of the boy 'Greg' which are in focus; the actions of the girls, here encoded in a verb marked with *-fooka,* provide a backdrop for his actions. I have translated the *-fooka-*marked verb with an English past perfect, a means in English of demoting a verb from the mainline.

In (89) *-fooka* occurs with past tense *-to*; it also occurs with the realis tense marker *-toho* in example (92) found later in this chapter.

(89) immayap   man   stacooka copalito:fookok
     immaya-p   man   stacooka co:pa-li-to-:fooka-k
     be^more-P again raffia   buy-1^SG^XR-PST^2-OFFLIN-K
     Next   raffia   having bought
     After I have bought raffia ...

In example (90) *-fooka* occurs on a stative verb and occurs with the distant past marker *-(k)kitta**, which is used like a tense suffix.

(90) paykahatkā imcaklilihcoolik
     cotton   I^used^to^chop^it

    cacoki:bosi:fookakkitto
    ca-co*:ba-ki-ō-si-:fooka-kkitta-to-˜
    1^SG^DO^STAT-be^big-3^NEG-3^NEG-DIM-OFFLIN-D^PST-PST-˜
    a long time ago when I was small
    I used to chop cotton long ago when I was young (not big).

Still, by Koasati standards, the morphology on *-fooka-*marked verbs is reduced. Most noteworthy is that *-hci* and *-fooka* are mutually exclusive; in this work I posit that -*hci* is a complementary marker of some element of discourse spectrum.[65]

The ±CONT markers which have been observed on -*fooka* are -*k*, -*n*, and -*p*, with -*w* occurring very rarely; -ˉ never occurs. Thus -*fooka* occurs in the word final forms given in (91).[66] As to distributional patterns, -*fooka* is an exception to what was stated in chapter three about nouns and verbs being similar in Koasati. The marker -*fooka* occurs exclusively on verbs.

(91)　The main forms of -*fooka*
　　　V-:*fookok*
　　　V-:*fookon*
　　　V-:*fookap*
　　　V-:*fookow*

Semantics. At first blush the suffix -*fooka* appears to mark contemporaneous time. Burnham (n.d.:6) and Kimball (1985:182–3) gloss it 'while, when', but Burnham further states that the suffix is a "means of inserting 'background information' into the sentence." The temporal significance of -*fooka* is only secondary: for various reasons, background and other kinds of offline information are frequently of contemporaneous time and can be translated with terms like 'while' and 'when'. Verbs marked with -*fooka* must sometimes be translated with English past tense forms as seen in example (88) above and in the following example, shortened and adapted from Kimball (1985:183).[67]

(92)　*mo:taho-k　pakaali-k　fayli-:fooka-o-k　ati-k*
　　　CONJ-K　　flower-K　　quit-OFFLIN-O-K　berry-K

　　　solotka-toho-:fooka-o-n　ipło-k　i:pa-Vhci
　　　dry-REAL-OFFLIN-O-N　squirrel-K　eat-ASP
　　　And then, after it has flowered out and then after its berries have dried, the squirrels eat them.

---

[65]Note for instance the alternation of -*hci* and -*fooka* in example (93).

[66]A suffix -*o* is added before all SR markers except -*p*, causing loss of final /a/. The same pattern of changes occurs with *aana** (1ˆSGˆPRO), *isna** (2ˆSGˆPRO), *ma** (3ˆPRO, deictic), and others. The addition of this suffix to these words or morphemes does not appear to have semantic import and is not marked in this work.

[67]Kimball glosses -*toho* REALIS; I have related this marker to tense. In the original this data was cited to illustrate that the suffix is "equivalent to the English words 'when' and 'while'."

5.2 The discourse function of *-fooka*: Spectrum

5.2.1. A Koasati text. In this section I look more closely at the discourse function of *-fooka* in a text in which the suffix occurs several times. This text provides a source of data for the discussion to follow. The interlinear data is added for completeness and reference; most of my comments refer to the two column spectrum translation which is in English and follows the interlinear data.

Text excerpt illustrating *-fooka*

Unit 21

matimhilkan	*tafilli:cit*	*hi:caayok*	
mat-im-ka-hilka-n	tafilli:ci-t	hi:ca-aya-o-k	
VIA-3^IO-give-1^PL^XR-N	turn^page-CONN	see-FRUS-O-K	
we gave it to him	he paged through it	he tried to see	

sami:caahik	*sobayko*	*maamoosin*	*naksofihnon*
sa:mi-:ci-aahi-k	sobayli-ko	maamoosi-n	nakso-fihna-o-n
happen-CAUS-INTN-K	know-3^NEG	CONJ-N	wherever-??-O-N
what to do	he didn't know	so then	where

imnali:kaahī	*immanhilkan*	*imnalihkok*	*yahopkaahosik*
im-nali:ka-aahi-ˉ	im-manka-hilka-n	im-nali:ka-h-o-k	yahopka-aahosi-k
3^IO-speak-INTN	3^IO-tell-1^PL^XR-N	3^IO-read-H-O-K	rejoice-very-K
he should read it	we showed him	reading it	he rejoiced

Romanian	*Bibleooliskan*	*imnali:kak*	*sobbaylik.*
Romanian	Bible-ooli-skan	im-nali:ka-k	sob*ayli-:-k
Romanian	Bible-ASP-CAUS	3^IO-speak-K	know-INTNS-K
Romanian	because it was a Bible	to read it	he knew how

We gave it to him, and he paged through it and tried to look at it but he did not know how, so we told him where to read and then reading it he was overjoyed because it was a Romanian Bible and he knew how to read it.

Unit 22

man	miiton	imnatikaahĩ	immanhilka:fookon	mon
man	miita-o-n	im-nati:ka-aahi-˜	im-manka-hilka-:fooka-n	ma-n
again	other-O-N	3^IO-read-INTN-˜	3^IO-tell-1^PL^XR-OFFLIN-N	3^PRO-N
next	other	he should read	we showing him	this also

man	imnati:ka:fookok	man	malmaamit	yahopkaahosik
man	im-nati:ka-:fooka-k	man	malmaami-t	yahopka-aahosi-k
again	3^IO-speak-OFFLIN-K	again	be^similar-CONN	rejoice-very-K
again	he^reading it	again	likewise	he rejoiced greatly

ma:min	mafa	immanhilkak	scikkihilka:fookon
ma:mi-n	ma-fa	im-manka-hilka-k	st-cikkika-hilka-:fooka-n
CONJ-N	3^PRO-LOC	3^IO-tell-1^PL^XR-K	INST-DU^sit-1^PL^XR-OFFLIN-N
but now	there	we showing him	we sitting with something

miita	mok	ilma:kat	itcokkahka:k	fayahkok
miita	ma-o-k	ilma:ka-t	it-cokka*:ka-h-k	fayahli-ko-k
other	3^PRO-O-K	come^PL-CONN	ILL-enter-H-K	quit^PL-3^NEG-K
others	these also	coming	entering in	not stop

alotkaahosit	ano:kak	roomkasik
alotka-aahosi-t	ano:ka-k	room-si-k
be^full-very-CONN	be^done-K	room-DIM-K
very full	it was	the room

coki:boshcooliskan
co:ba-ki-o-si-hci-ooli-skan
be^big-3^NEG^XR-NEG-DIM-ASP-ASP-CAUS
since it was small

Once again as we told him [where] to read and when he also read these, once again in the same way he rejoiced. So while we were sitting there showing him like this, others continued coming in with the result that the little room got very full since it was so small.

Unit 23

ma:min   immayan   chapterkoot   versekoot   imwihlit
ma:mi-n   immaya-n   chapter-oot   verse-oot   im-wihli-t
CONJ-N   be^more-N   chapter-SER   verse-SER   3^IO-look^for-CONN
and   more   chapters   verses   looking for

immanhilka:fookon   caffaakat   imimnałi:ka:fookon
im-manka-hilka-:fooka-n   caffaaka-t   im-im-nałi:ka-:fooka-n
3^IO-tell-1^PL^XR-OFFLIN-N   be^one-CONN   3^IO-3^IO-speak-OFFLIN-N
we showing them   one   he reading them to the people

aati   ohyak   ittimmankat   ittimasilha:cit
aati   ohya-k   ittim-manka-t   i ttim-asilha:ci-t
person   be^all-K   RECIP-tell-CONN   RECIP-ask-CONN
person   everything   talk together   ask one another

sti:saahosik   ilbootahon   ohya   sfamohkat
st-i:sa-aahosi-k   ilbi-taho-n   ohya   st-famohka-t
INST-AUX^keep^on-very-K   hand-PST-N   be^all   INST-wave-CONN
they kept on at this   hands   everything   they waved

pahkat   sti:saamoolik
pahka-t   st-i:sa-:mooli-k
yell-CONN   INST-AUX^keep^on-??-K
yell   they kept on and on

So when we selected and showed them more chapters and verses and one person read them, all the people talked with one another and asked one another questions and waved their arms and yelled on and on.

Unit 24

[Arbitrarily left out]

Unit 25

ilhi:cak   skomkanaahosik
il-hi:ca-k   st-kom-kaano-aahosi-k
1^PL^XR-see-K   INST-1^PL^IO^STAT-be^good-very-K
we saw   it was good to us (we liked it)

ohimalosti:fookon   *stakoyokpaahosik*
oh-im-alosti-:fooka-n   st-ko-a#yokpa-aahosi-k[68]
3^PL-3^IO^STAT-enjoy-OFFLIN-N   INST-1^PL^DO^STAT-like-very-K
it pleasing them (they liked it) we rejoiced greatly

Watching them was a joy for us because they liked it and we rejoiced in this.

5.2.2. A translation indicating spectrum. This section presents a special translation designed to help analyze the function of *-fooka* in the above text: verbs with and without *-fooka* are segregated, so that those which are suffixed with *-fooka* occur bolded in the right column,[69] and those without occur in the left column. ±CONT markers are left untranslated and the suffix *-fooka* is represented by F. Koasati word order is strictly followed. Line numbers will be referred to in the discussion; unit numbers cross-reference to the interlinear text.

```
 1    Unit 21:
 2    (the Bible) we^give^him-N
 3    page^through-T try^to^see-K
 4    what^to^do^so-K he^does^not^know so-N
 5    where he^can^read-⁻ we^show^him-N
 6    reading^it-K he^rejoice-K Romanian
 7    Bible^since^it^is to^read^it-K
 8    he^really^understand-K
 9                            Unit 22:
10                            again more-N which^he^can^read-⁻
11                            we^show^him-F-N this^also-N
12                            again he^read^it-F-K
13    now again in^the^same^way-T
14    he^rejoice-K
15    so-N there we^show^him-K
16                            we^sit^there^with^him-F-N
17    others also-K come-T enter-K
```

---

[68]The symbol # is used to mark the location of an infixed prefix. In this instance, *ko* is the infixed first-plural direct-object prefix with the root *a#yokpa* 'like'. At times, there may be two prefixes occurring in this manner of infixation (cf. example (94) on page 70).

[69]Two verbs in the right column are not themselves marked with *-fooka:* 'read' (line 10) and 'seek' (line 23). However, these verbs are syntactically and semantically linked to the following *-fooka*-marked verbs; for instance 'read' is the embedded object of 'show-F-N,' and 'seek' is linked to 'show-F-N' with the connector *-t*.

Spectrum, -*Fooka*, and Switch Reference

```
18    they^not^stop-K it^is^very^full-T
19    is^completely-K the^little^room-K
20    since^it^was^small
21                    Unit 23:
22                    so-N more-N chapter-T verse-T
23                    seek^them-T we^show^them-F-N
24                    one^person-T
25                    read^them^to^them-F-N
26    people all-K talk^together-T
27    ask^one^another-T they^keep^on-K
28    arms-N everything wave^them-T
29    yell-T they^keep^on^and^on-K
30    Unit 25:
31    we^see-K it^is^good^to^us-K
32                    they^are^happy-F-N
33    we^rejoice-K
```

5.2.3. Discussion of text. Note first of all that none of the verbs which appear in the right column introduce new information or action. The verb 'show' in the right column (line 11) appeared first in the left column (line 5); 'read' in the right column (line 12) appeared first in the left column (lines 5–7); 'sit' in the right column (line 16) appeared in the discourse before Unit 21; and so forth. The -*fooka* suffix is appended only to verbs which do not advance the action of the discourse.

Again, the secondary nature of the verbs marked by -*fooka* can be seen by reading the two columns separately. A coherent, though somewhat jumpy story is maintained by the left column. On the other hand the right column alone is quite sketchy, both referentially and in terms of action. A chunk of new information (frequently a new event) is introduced in the left column (i.e., without -*fooka*) and then the chunk is echoed or reformulated or anchored in the listener's mind in the right column (i.e., with -*fooka*). This echo function, often seen in a very transparent form as in example (93), is referred to by Longacre (1983b:9) as "tail-head linkage."

(93) asaala sco:palihcho sco:pali:fookok casnaahot
asaala sco:pa-li-hci sco:pa-li-:fooka-k ca-snaaho-t
Baskets I^sell^them I^sell^them-OFFLIN-K I^rich

    anookallaho
    anooka-li-laho
    I^will^become

I sell baskets and, selling them, I will get rich [said facetiously by a Koasati lady].

In such examples *-fooka* functions to back-reference or maintain cohesion; Longacre (1989) assigns this function to the lowest band in the English spectrum. An example of another kind of offline information is seen in line 16 where the *-fooka*-marked verb (we^sit^there^with^him-F-N) provides setting.

This overview of the discourse function of *-fooka* enables us to now discuss the interaction of ±CONT marking and the demoting effect of *-fooka*.

5.3 ±CONT marking and *-fooka*

There are environments in which a number of verbs, conjunctions, and verbs marked with *-fooka* occur in an involved chain. This creates a situation in which complex and/or exceptional SR marking can potentially occur if the right conditions of subject switch obtain. This is harder to follow in the abstract than it is with actual data—see (94).

(94) nashollomahcoot naasi santik i:sā
nashollo-mami-hci-oot naasi santi-k i:sa-⁻
wild-DUB-ASP-SER whatever whatever-K live^PL-⁻
whatever is wild whatever everything be^alive

    ittimapotknannan tayyon naanon stoklon
    ittim-apotka-nanna-n tayyi-n naani-n st-toklo-n
    RECIP-be^beside-many-N female-N male-N INST-be^two-N
    side by side female male both

    matcimtohnollahō ma:min naasi
    cim-∅-mat##ohno-li-lahō ma:mi-n naasi
    2^SG^IO-3DO-send^out-1^SG^XR-FUT^1 CONJ-N something
    I will send them to you and any kind of

Spectrum, -*Fooka*, and Switch Reference

wayooka mok malma:min
wayooka ma-o-k malma:mi-n
bird 3^PRO-O-K likewise-N
bird these likewise

matcimtohnoli:fookon piłafa
cim-∅-mat##tohno-li-:fooka-n piła-fa
2^SG^IO-3DO-send^out-1^SG^XR-OFFLIN-N boat-LOC
I sending them to you boat

ohya matałī
ohyā mat-ałi-¯
be^all VIA-load-DELAY
all (you) load them up
... wild animals—everything that is alive—side by side, males and females I will send to you and (*ma:min*) everything which flies this also I likewise sending to you (and then [delayed imperative] you) load them all into the boat.

This sentence fragment is best discussed with a "spectrum display," which allows us to see graphically that *-fooka*-marked verbs add a vertical dimension to Koasati discourse. In figure (95) (and all the spectrum displays in the remainder of this chapter) the original clause order is maintained by reading strictly from left to right, i.e., the elevated clause (beginning with "everything") occurs between the lower two clauses. The arrows indicate the two verbs which are related by the given SR marker.

(95) Spectrum display (a)

everything that flies I^send-F-N
|
animals I^will^send *ma:mi*-N ─────────── (you) load^them all

Note that the marking *-n* on *ma:mi** 'and' appears to be exceptional when viewed from a linear model. But this *-n* is not marking the relationship with the offline information immediately following the verb I^send-F-N, but rather with the mainline verb ('load them up!'). The demoted information leads, as it were, a shadowy existence, and the SR marking shoots through it and links with mainline material. Example (96) (from Unit 25) illustrates this phenomenon again.

(96) ilhi:cak   skomkanaahosik
      il-hi:ca-k   st-kom-kaano-aahosi-k
      1ˆPLˆXR-see-K   INST-1ˆPLˆIOˆSTAT-beˆgood-very-K
      we see   we are happy

    ohimalosti:fookon   stakoyokpaahosik
    oh-im-alosti-:fooka-n   st-ko-a#yokpa-aahosi-k
    3ˆPL-3ˆIOˆSTAT-please-OFFLIN-N INST-1ˆPLˆDOˆSTAT-love-very-K
    they being pleased   we rejoice

Watching them we were happy (because) they liked it and we rejoiced in this.

Again in a spectrum diagram:

(97) Spectrum display (b)

                        theyˆareˆpleased-F-N
                                     ↓
weˆsee-K weˆareˆveryˆhappy-K ⟶ weˆloveˆitˆveryˆmuch-K

Here again the (first) ±CONT marking, -k, shoots through the offline information and links mainline with mainline.[70]

This process becomes more complicated with the addition of more verbs marked by -fooka, creating a situation in which two parallel continuity referencing processes proceed independently of one another, i.e., one on the offline verbs and one on the mainline verbs. Example (98) nearly exemplifies this situation, except that -p, which is little understood but clearly does not have subject tracing semantics, occurs in the spot of the ±CONT markers.

(98) hayo   Maryk   hicak   scokkolik   ma:min
      hayō   Mary-k   hi*:ca-∅-k   st-cokko:li-k ma:mi-n
      inside Mary-K   see-DBLT-K   INST-sit-K   CONJ-N
      inside Mary   looking   she sit with it and

---

[70]Here we are not dealing with strictly mainline information. All three verbs are experiential-state verbs, and mainline verbs are typically action verbs. On the other hand, addition of the intensive suffix -aahosi* 'very' may promote the verbs to mainline.

Spectrum, -*Fooka*, and Switch Reference 73

> *hicak   scokkoli:fookap   aati   caffaakat*
> *hi*:ca-∅-k   st-cokko:li-:fooka-p   aati   caffaaka-t*
> see-DBLT-K   INST-sit-OFFLIN-P   person be^one-T
> looking   she sitting with it   person one

> *acā   ɬopotli:fookok   okhicasifa   mathi:cak*
> *aca   ɬopotli-:fooka-k   okhicasi-fa   mat-hi:ca-k*
> outside pass^by-OFFLIN-K   window-LOC   DIST-see-K
> outside as he was going by   thru the window   he looked in
> ... inside Mary sat looking at it, and while she was sitting looking
> [at it], a man walking by outside looked in through the window ...

Again, this is best seen in a spectrum display.

(99)   Spectrum display (c): two levels

$$
\begin{array}{c}
?? \\
\text{look-K sit\textasciicircum with-F-P} \longrightarrow \text{man-T go\textasciicircum by-F-K} \\
\downarrow \\
\text{Mary-K look-K sit-K } ma{:}mi\text{-N} \longrightarrow \text{he\textasciicircum look\textasciicircum in-K}
\end{array}
$$

The linear order of this example would make the -*n* marking on *ma:mi** extremely exceptional: it would imply that 'look-K sit' *(hicak scokko:lik)* and 'look-K sit-F' *(hicak scokko:li-:fookak)* are different in subject—but they are identical in terms of reference, continuity, and semantics, and except for -*fooka* they are identical morphologically. Again with the diagram we can visualize that the conjunction *ma:mi** and the -*n* marking are connecting the two mainline verbs *scokko:lik* and *mathi:cak* which are –CONT. The clauses which are offline are above the SR activity; it is not certain what the marking is doing on that level.

In example (100), taken from Unit 22, we again find two distinct levels of SR marking except for the presence of a sentence boundary.

(100) *sob:aylik]*   man   miiton   *imnaɬikaahī*
       sob:ayli-k]   man   miita-o-n   *im-naɬi:ka-aahi-ˉ*
       prior sentence]   again other-O-N   3^IO-read-INTN-ˉ
       he understand]   again other   he should read

```
            immanhilka:fookon            mon         man  imnati:ka:fookok
            im-manka-hilka-:fooka-n      ma-o-n      man  im-nati:ka-:fooka-k
            3^IO-tell-1^PL^XR-OFFLIN-N   3^PRO-O-N   again 3^IO-read-OFFLIN-K
            we telling him               this also   again he reading it

            himaya  man    malmaamit       yahopkaahosik
            himaya  man    malmaamit       yahopka-aahosi-k
            now     again  be^similar      rejoice-very-K
            now     again  likewise        he rejoiced
```
... he understood.] When we showed him other places to read and when he read these once again, he once again likewise was exceedingly pleased.

In an illustrated form:[71]

(101) Spectrum display (d): two levels

```
            we^tell^him-F-N  ─────────▶  he^read^it-F-K
                                                │
            [he^understand-K]                he^rejoiced-K
```

The -*n* marking on the verb 'we tell' relates to 'he read,' and the -*k* marking on the latter offline verb relates to the mainline verb 'he rejoices'. The mainline arrow has not been drawn in as it is not clear whether the -*k* marking on 'he understands*' relates to 'he rejoices' due to the presence of a sentence boundary.[72]

Example (102) is similar to (100) in that what appears to be a sentence boundary precedes the sentence-initial conjunction *maamoosi*-N.

```
(102)  Noahk  pita  talibo:lit       stati:yatoolimpahco      maamoosin
       Noah-k pita  talibo:li-t      sta-ti:ya-toolimpa-hci-o maamoosi-n
       Noah-K boat  make-CONN        INST-go-NARRA-ASP-O      CONJ-N
       Noah   boat  make             he went about            so then
```

---

[71]Several words occurring as arguments have been dropped in this figure including the verb *imnatikaahī* which here serves as the object of *immanhilka:fookon*.

[72]This -*k* may be the -*ki* discussed in chapter one, footnote 11, though I tend to view it as a SR marker. Nevertheless, the ±CONT marking on conjunctions does function across sentence boundaries.

Spectrum, -*Fooka*, and Switch Reference

piła talibo:lit   stałi:ya:fookok   ommi:k   Noahk
piła talibo:li-t   st-ałi:ya-:fooka-k   ommi-k   Noah-k
boat make-CONN   INST-go-OFFLIN-2OM   AUX-K   Noah-K
boat make   he going about   emphasis   Noah

aatimayba:cit   naasi   acihbahcok   i:laahī
aatim-ayba:ci-t   naasi   acihba-hci-k   i:la-aahi-˜
HUM^IO-warn-CONN   something   be^bad-ASP-K   arrive^there-INTN-˜
warn people   something   terrible   will come

immankat   stałiya:fookon   ohafa:li:citoolimpahcok   piila
im-manka-t   st-ałi:ya-:fooka-n   oh-afa:li:ci-toolimpa-hci-k   piila
3^IO-tell-CONN   INST-go-OFFLIN-N   3^PL-laugh^at-NARRA-ASP-K   just
tell them   he going about   they laughed at him   just

Noah went about making the boat. So now as he went about making the boat and as Noah (went about) warning the people "Something bad is going to come," he went about telling them, they just laughed at him.

The three verbs suffixed with *-t* (CONN) form verbal doublets with different forms of the verb *stałi:ya* and do not play a part in the SR marking because they are immediately linked to the latter for all their person, number, and ±CONT marking. In the spectrum display they occur as V-T. The relevant words are displayed in example (103).

(103) Spectrum display (e): two levels

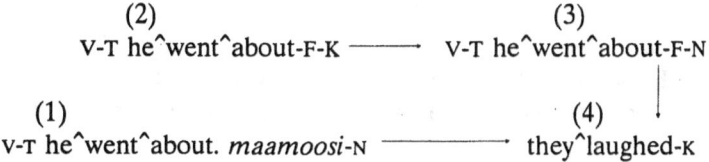

Note that the first clause (1) and the last (4) are separated by eleven words, so that the discontinuity marked by the first *-n* (occurring here as *maamoosin*) is delayed a significant time. This is a stylistic means of creating tension and highlighting the contrast between Noah's steady obedience and the people's irresponsible behavior. Another stylistic device common in Koasati is the repeated use of a vocabulary item; this feature also is seen in the threefold repetition of the helping verb *ałi:ya* 'to go on'.

Conclusion regarding ±CONT marking and *-fooka*. In chapter four I argued that some *-k* and *-n* marking which is exceptional from the perspective of canonical SR can be explained with reference to the more abstract concept of ±CONT. In this chapter I have argued that other exceptional marking can be explained with reference to the discourse notion of spectrum. This leads us to the question: what would happen if both of these complex and abstract conditions obtained in one verbal chain? In other words, what if (1) two mainline verbs were separated by a *-fooka*-marked verb, and (2) the two mainline verbs were in a conflicting condition such as discussed in chapter four, namely, +CONT and DS or −CONT and SS? What marking would appear, *-k* or *-n*? Such a situation would be very rare, since either condition alone is rare. One possible example is given below.

5.4 Some reflections

At some point in this argument the reader may have had his or her credulity stretched. Can Koasati speakers actually be making such exacting decisions about how they are going to mark a sentence for SR and ±CONT? Such reservations have merit, and I make some equivocations about the state of my analysis and present some counter-examples in §5.5. On the other hand, I can present anecdotal evidence which indicates that speakers are thinking sentences and clauses ahead in processing SR marking.

When producing lengthy or pragmatically complex sentences, speakers sometimes have difficulty choosing appropriate SR marking. One person who was learning to read Koasati was reading a story he had told earlier and came to the following section which included a sentence boundary.

(104) *Eltonfa   aliswahcoolik   mootahok Baton Rougekafa antiyak* ...
      in Elton   we were living and   to Baton Rouge we went
      We were living at the time in Elton. Then we went to Baton Rouge.

In reading this he initially produced *mootahon* (an erroneous reading for *mootahok*) and read on to the end of the line cited. He then paused for four seconds, revised his reading to *mootahok*, and went on. Such misreadings occurred not infrequently.

Furthermore, I find in my data exceptional markings which I am unable to explain at all; I suspect that some of these exceptions are due to performance errors caused by the complexity of the process. In fact, in editing and analyzing texts, language consultants occasionally changed SR marking which they had made in earlier recordings or transcriptions. Or sometimes the ±CONT marking in a text gathered from one consultant would be unacceptable to another consultant helping me with that text. It has usually been difficult to determine if the disagreement was due to dialect differences,[73] misunderstanding of pragmatics, or other factors; consultants often are unable to explain why one form is correct and the other incorrect. Due to a community-wide sensitivity about proper Koasati, I usually avoided long discussion of such matters.

5.5 Counter-examples

From the way I have presented the data thus far, it would appear that chains with *-fooka* are always neatly divided into different levels. This is not always the case, and I now give some counter-examples in which SR and *-fooka*-marked verbs do not behave as described above. The man telling the story in example (105) had been in the woods felling trees and was not aware that he was standing on a wasp nest.

(105) *mootoliiyan   anok   sikli:cit   nahholok*
       mootoliiyan   ano-k   sikli-:ci-t   na*:ho-h-li-k
       CONJ   1ˆSGˆPRO-K   saw-CAUS-CONN   do-H-1ˆSGˆXR-K
       meantime (?)   I   use saw   I was going about

   koyoffila:fookok   matimpahacca:lili:fookon
   koyli-li-:fooka-k   mat-im-pa-hacca:li-li-:fooka-n
   cutˆPL-1ˆSGˆXR-OFFLIN-K   VIA-3ˆIO-upon-stand-ˆ1ˆSGˆXR-OFFLIN-N
   I cutting   I standing there right on top of them

   askahkato   foolaanakok
   achhali:ka-to   foolaana-ka-o-k
   comeˆoutˆPL-PST   wasp-??-O-K
   they came out   those wasps

So in the meantime I for my part was sawing away and, while I was cutting... while I was standing right upon [the wasp hole], the wasps came out.

A spectrum display of this chain looks different from those above.

---

[73]There are dialect variations among the 200 speakers in Elton, Louisiana.

(106) Display with no spectrum

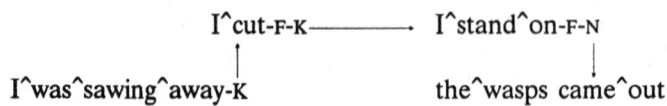

Here the SR marking follows a linear model, rather than reflecting features of spectrum, and the mainline verbs cannot be connected by an arrow. The text in (105) occurs at "peak" which may have some bearing on the marking.[74] It is also possibile that the -*k* on the first verb might suggest a CAUSAL CONNECTION between the 'sawing' and the 'wasps coming out'. Thus the correct display would be:

(107) Display *with* spectrum

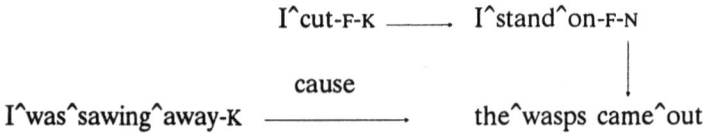

Here the arrow connecting the mainline verbs does not indicate ±CONT (+CONT in this case since I^was^sawing^away* is marked with -K) of subject, but rather ±CONT (+CONT) of causality. Thus, this may be an example of the doubly complex situation postulated at the end of §5.3.

5.6 Conclusion

In this chapter I have explained exceptional marking by resorting to an abstract external concept from textual studies, viz., that of spectrum. The suffix -*fooka* demotes verbs away from the mainline, and ±CONT marking is sensitive to this feature of Koasati discourse. Future research in extensive discourse material can refine these statements and enhance our appreciation of features of Koasati discourse and of the pivotal role which the ±CONT marking system has in all features of the language.

---

[74]Suggested as a possibility by Hwang. In Longacre 1985b "Discourse peak as zone of turbulence," he argues that grammatical rules which otherwise hold true can be suspended at the peak of a story. I have observed this to be the case with Koasati SR marking as has Burnham (p.c.).

References

Burnham, Gene. n.d. The deep and surface structures of Koasati sentences. ms.

Comrie, Bernard. 1981. Language universals and linguistic typology. Chicago: University of Chicago.

———. 1983. Switch-reference in Huichol: A typological study. In Haiman and Munro (eds.), 17–38.

———. 1987. Grammatical relations, semantic roles and topic-comment structure in a New Guinea highland language: Harway. In Ross Steele and Terry Threadgold (eds.), Language topics: Essays in honour of Michael Halliday, 355–66. Amsterdam: John Benjamins.

———. 1988. Switch reference in Harway: Grammar or discourse? Paper presented at the Linguistics Forum of the University of Texas Arlington and the Summer Institute of Linguistics, October, 1988. Arlington, Texas.

Crystal, David. 1985. Dictionary of linguistics and phonetics. Oxford: Basil Blackwell.

Davies, William D. 1981. Choctaw switch reference and levels of syntactic representation. Linguistic Notes from La Jolla 9:79–101. San Diego: Department of Linguistics, University of California.

———. 1982. A semantic contribution to Choctaw referential coding phenomena. Kansas Working Papers in Linguistics 7:31–48.

Davis, Philip W. and Heather K. Hardy. 1984. Nominal-sentential morphology in Alabama. Southwest Journal of Linguistics 7:87–101.

―― and ――. 1985. Centrality and peripherality as explanatory hypotheses. ms.

―― and ――. 1986. Alabama relative clauses. ms.

―― and ――. 1987. The *ist-* prefix in Alabama. ms.

―― and ――. 1988. Absence of noun marking in Alabama. International Journal of American Linguistics 54:279–308.

Dooley, Robert A. 1989. Switch reference in Mbya Guarani: A fair-weather phenomenon. In Dooley and Bickford (eds.), 93–119.

―― and J. Albert Bickford, eds. 1989. Workpapers of the Summer Institute of Linguistics University of North Dakota 33. Dallas: Summer Institute of Linguistics.

Evans, Bergen and Cornelia Evans. 1957. A dictionary of contemporary American usage. New York: Random House. Quoted in Arthur Plotnik, 1982, The elements of editing: A modern guide for editors and journalists, 45. New York: Collier MacMillan.

Foley, William A. and Robert D. Van Valin, Jr. 1980. Role and reference grammar. In Edith Moravscik and J. Wirth (eds.), Current approaches to syntax, 329–53. New York: Academic Press.

―― and ――. 1984. Functional syntax and universal grammar. Cambridge: Cambridge University Press.

Franklin, Karl J. 1983. Some features of interclausal reference in Kewa. In Haiman and Munro (eds.), 39–49.

Givón, Talmy. 1979. On understanding grammar. New York: Academic Press.

――, ed. 1983a. Topic continuity in discourse: Quantitative cross-language studies. Typological Studies in Language 1. Amsterdam: John Benjamins.

――. 1983b. Topic continuity in discourse: The functional domain of switch-reference. In Haiman and Munro (eds.), 51–82.

――. 1984. Syntax: A functional-typological approach, Vol. 1. Amsterdam: John Benjamins.

Gordon, Lynn. 1979. *-k* and *-m* in Maricopa. In Munro (ed.), 119–43.

――. 1983. Switch reference, clause order, and interclausal relationships in Maricopa. In Haiman and Munro (eds.), 83–104.

――. 1987. Relative clauses in Western Muskogean languages. In Munro (ed.), 66–80.

Grimes, Joseph E. 1975. The thread of discourse. The Hague: Mouton.

Haas, Mary R. 1941. The classification of the Muskogean languages. In Leslie Spier, A. Irving Hallowell, and Stanley S. Newman (eds.), Language, culture and personality: Essays in memory of Edward Sapir, 41–56. Menasha, Wisconsin: Sapir Memorial Publication Fund.

References

―――. 1944. Men's and women's speech in Koasati. Language 20:142–9.
―――. 1946. A proto-Muskogean paradigm. Language 22:326–32.
Haiman, John and Pamela Munro, eds. 1983. Switch-reference and universal grammar. Proceedings of a Symposium on Switch Reference and Universal Grammar, Winnipeg, May 1981. Amsterdam: John Benjamins.
Hardy, Heather. 1982. Pragmatics and the syntax of switch reference in Tolkapaya. Southwest Journal of Linguistics 5:85–99.
――― and Philip W. Davis. 1988. Comparatives in Alabama. International Journal of American Linguistics 54:209–31.
――― and ―――. 1989. The semantics of agreement in Alabama. ms.
――― and Timothy R. Montler. 1988. Imperfective gemination in Alabama. International Journal of American Linguistics 54:399–415.
Healey, Phyllis. 1966. Levels and chaining in Telefol sentences. Pacific Linguistics B-5. Canberra: Department of Linguistics, Australian National University.
Heath, Jeffrey. 1977. Choctaw cases. Berkeley Linguistics Society 3:204–13.
Hopper, Paul J. 1979. Aspect and foregrounding in discourse. In Talmy Givón (ed.), Discourse and syntax, 213–41. Syntax and Semantics 12. New York: Academic Press.
――― and S. A. Thompson. 1980. Transitivity in grammar and discourse. Language 56:251–99.
Hwang, Shin Ja Joo. 1989. Recursion in the paragraph as a unit of discourse development. Discourse Processes 12:461–77.
―――. 1990. Foreground information in narrative. Southwest Journal of Linguistics. 9:2:63–90.
Hymes, Dell, and W. Bittle, eds. 1967. Studies in Southwestern ethnolinguistics: Meaning and history in the languages of the American Southwest. Studies in General Anthropology 3. The Hague: Mouton.
Jacobsen, William H., Jr. 1967. Switch-reference in Hokan-Coahuiltecan. In Dell Hymes and W. Bittle (eds.), Studies in southwestern ethnolinguistics: Meaning and history in the languages of the American Southwest, 238–63. Studies in General Anthropology 3. The Hague: Mouton.
―――. 1983. Typological and genetic notes on switch reference systems in North America. In Haiman and Munro (eds.), 151–84.
Jacobson, Daniel, Howard N. Martin, and Ralph Henry Marsh. 1974. (Creek) Indians: Alabama-Coushatta. New York: Garland.
Johnson, Bobby. 1976. The Coushatta people. Phoenix: Indian Tribal Series.

Jones, Larry B. and Linda K. Jones. 1979. Multiple levels of information in discourse. In Jones (ed.), 3–28.

Jones, Linda K., ed. 1979. Discourse studies in Mesoamerican languages 1: Discussion. Summer Institute of Linguistics and the University of Texas at Arlington publications in linguistics 58.1. Dallas.

Jones, Roy G. 1986. The semantics of -o- in Coushatta. In Mary C. Marino and Luis A. Perez (eds.), The twelfth LACUS forum 1985, 306–13. Lake Bluff, Illinois: The Linguistics Association of Canada and the United States.

Kendall, Martha B. 1975. The /-k/, /-m/ problem in Yavapai syntax. International Journal of American Linguistics 41:1–9.

Kimball, Geoffrey. 1982. Koasati word list. Computer printout.

———. 1985. A descriptive grammar of Koasati. Ph.D. dissertation, Tulane University. Ann Arbor, Michigan: University Microfilms.

———. 1990. Koasati grammar. Lincoln, Nebraska: University of Nebraska.

Langdon, Margaret and Pamela Munro. 1976. Subject and (switch) reference in Yuman. ms.

——— and ———. 1979. Subject and (switch-) reference in Yuman. Folia Linguistica 3:321–44.

Linker, Wendy. 1987. On the coordinating status of the switch-reference markers *chah* and *nah* in Choctaw. In Munro (ed.), 96–110.

Litteral, Robert. 1987. Classroom lecture on the SR system of Anggor. University of Texas at Arlington.

Longacre, Robert E. 1976. The discourse structure of the flood narrative. In George MacRae (ed.), Society of Biblical Literature, 1976 seminar papers. Missoula, Montana: Scholars.

———. 1977. A discourse manifesto. Notes on Linguistics 4:17–29. Dallas: Summer Institute of Linguistics.

———. 1981. A spectrum and profile approach to discourse analysis. Text 1:332–59.

———. 1983a. Switch-reference systems in two distinct linguistic areas: Wojokeso (Papua New Guinea) and Guanano (South America). In Haiman and Munro (eds.), 185–207.

———. 1983b. The grammar of discourse. New York: Plenum.

———. 1984. Switch-reference and subject raising in Seri. In Eung-Do Cook and Donna B. Gerdts (eds.), The syntax of Native American languages, 247–68. Syntax and Semantics 16. New York: Academic Press.

———. 1985a. Sentences as combinations of clauses. In Shopen (ed.), 2:235–86.

References

———. 1985b. Discourse peak as zone of turbulence. In Wirth (ed.), 81-105.

———. 1989. Two hypotheses regarding text generation and analysis. Discourse Processes 12:413–60.

Moser, Mary B. 1978. Switch-reference in Seri. International Journal of American Linguistics 44:113–20.

Munro, Pamela, ed. 1979a. Studies of switch-reference. UCLA Papers in Syntax 8. Los Angeles: University of California at Los Angeles.

———. 1979b. A questionnaire on switch-reference. In Munro (ed.), 1979a:45.

———. 1979c. On the syntactic status of switch-reference clauses: The special case of Mojave comitatives. In Munro (ed.), 1979a:144–59.

———. 1980a. Three tests for subjecthood in Chickasaw. Paper presented at the Southwestern Anthropological Association Meeting, San Diego.

———. 1980b. Mojave k and m: It ain't necessarily so. In Redden (ed.), 124–9.

———. 1983. When "same" is not "not different." In Haiman and Munro (eds.), 223–43.

———, ed. 1987. Muskogean linguistics. UCLA Occasional Papers In Linguistics 6. Los Angeles: University of California at Los Angeles.

——— and Lynn Gordon. 1982. Syntactic relations in western Muskogean: A typological perspective. Language 58:81–115.

Nathan, Michele. 1980. Switch-reference in Seminole. Abstract of paper presented at the Conference on Muskogean Languages and Linguistics. International Journal of American Linguistics 46:44.

O'Connor, Catherine. 1981. Northern Pomo switch-reference and subject case-marking: Functional competition and formal compromise. Paper presented at the Conference on the Syntax of Native American Languages, University of Calgary.

Payne, Doris L. 1979. Switch-reference in Chickasaw. In Munro (ed.), 89–118.

———. 1982. Chickasaw agreement morphology: A functional explanation. In Paul Hopper and Sandra Thompson (eds.), Studies in transitivity, 351–78. New York: Academic Press.

Redden, James, ed. 1980. Proceedings of the 1979 Hokan languages workshop. Occasional Papers on Linguisitics 7. Carbondale, Illinois: Department of Linguisitics, Southern Illinois University.

———. 1980. On Walapai /-k/ and /-m/. In Redden (ed.), 68–71.

Sadock, Jerrold M. and Arnold M. Zwicky. 1985. Speech act distinctions in syntax. In Shopen (ed.), 1:155–96.

Sander, Gerald and Jessica R. Wirth. 1985. Discourse, pragmatics, and linguistic form. In Wirth (ed.), 1–20.

Schachter, Paul. 1985. Parts-of-speech systems. In Shopen (ed.), 1:361.

Schuetze-Coburn, Stephan. 1987. Exceptional *t/n*-marking in Oklahoma Seminole Creek. In Munro (ed.), 146–59.

Shopen, Timothy, ed. 1985. Language typology and syntactic description, 3 vols. Cambridge: Cambridge University Press.

Simons, Gary F. and Larry Versaw. 1988. How to use IT. Dallas: Summer Institute of Linguistics.

Slater, Carol E. 1977. The semantics of switch-reference in Kwtsaan. Berkeley Linguistics Society 3:24–35.

Thompson, Sandra A. 1987. "Subordination" and narrative event structure. In R. S. Tomlin (ed.), Cohesion and grounding in discourse, 435–54. Typological Studies in Language 11. Amsterdam: John Benjamins.

―――― and Robert E. Longacre. 1985. Adverbial clauses. In Shopen (ed.), 2:171–234.

Tomlin, Russell S. 1985. Foreground-background information and the syntax of subordination. Text 5:85–122.

Todd, Terry Lynn. 1975. Clause versus sentence in Choctaw. Linguistics 161:39–67.

Watkins, Laurel J. 1978. Subject, topic, and switch reference in Kiowa. In Ralph Cooley, Mervin R. Barnes, and John A Dunn (eds.), Proceedings of the 1978 Mid-America linguistics conference, 32–43. Norman: University of Oklahoma.

――――. 1987. Switch-reference in Kiowa discourse. In M. T. Henderson (ed.), 1987 Mid-America linguistics conference papers, 319–26. Lawrence, Kansas: University of Kansas.

Wirth, Jessica R., ed. 1985. Beyond the sentence: Discourse and sentential form. Ann Arbor: Karoma.

Index

action continuity 57

back-reference 62, 70
background information 62, 64

canonical 2–3, 12–13, 36, 76
case 6–11, 14, 32, 36, 38, 41–46, 48–50, 56–58
centrality 42
chain 24, 28, 32–37, 42, 57, 70, 76–77
  chain embedding 34–37
clause 4, 7–8, 22, 33–38, 49, 53–55, 57, 60, 71, 73, 75–76
  adjectival 34
  adverbial 60
  relative 8, 34–37
conjunction 5, 24, 33, 35, 54, 70, 73–74
conjunctive word 7, 24, 55
continuity 5, 13–14, 23–24, 26–28, 32–33, 35, 37–38, 41, 43–44, 46–47, 49–59, 62, 64, 68, 70, 72–78
control 25, 28, 56

demotion 62
discontinuity 13–14, 53, 55, 57, 73, 75
discourse 58–60, 71, 78

exceptional marking 5, 12, 14, 22, 36, 59, 76, 78
expectancy reversal 48, 52

explanation
  external 23
  internal 23

functional 3, 5, 13, 24, 34, 36, 42

hierarchy 32–33

inertia 57–58
information 3, 10–11, 14, 22, 24, 38, 41–49, 55–60, 62, 64, 69–72
  flow of 42, 57
  new 42–44, 46, 48, 56, 69
  old 38, 43, 48–49, 56
  type 41, 43, 45, 48, 56, 58, 62

k om 50, 52–53

length 18

mainline 55, 61–63, 71–74, 76, 78

n om 50–53
nasalization 2–3, 8–9, 17, 34, 43
nominal marking 7, 42
noun phrase 36, 38

object 3, 10, 18–19, 29, 32, 34–38, 41–42, 47–50, 56, 62, 68, 74
oblique cases 43
oblique marking 7, 48

offline 55, 64, 70–74
ommi 9, 45, 48, 50–53, 55, 75

part of speech 23, 27, 42
participant tracing 5
peripherality 42
pragmatic 14, 22–23, 32, 47–48, 56, 58, 76–77
prominence 60
pronoun 3–4, 27, 36, 48

reduction 43
role 2–3, 7–8, 13, 21, 24, 26–27, 29, 34, 49, 58, 78

spectrum 59–62, 65, 68, 70–78
statistics 11
  statistical 3, 14, 27, 44–45
subject 3–5, 9, 13–14, 22–23, 26–32, 35–38, 41–51, 54–56, 58, 61–62, 70, 72–73

different 4, 9, 13–14, 22, 35, 53–54, 58, 73, 76
same 4, 9–11, 13–14, 34–39, 43–48, 50–55, 57–58, 76
subject set 22, 47, 54
subject switch 5, 37, 70
switch reference 2, 3, 5, 9, 11, 14, 18, 21–28, 32–33, 36–39, 41, 49, 53, 56, 58, 70–71, 73–78

topic continuity 13, 57
type I 29–30, 32
type II 29–30, 32
type III 29–30, 32

verb 3–5, 14, 18, 22–33, 35–38, 41–42, 44–47, 49–50, 52–60, 62–65, 68–78
  active 28–31, 45
  stative 29, 60
verbal chains 28, 32
verbal morphology 23–24, 27
volition 28–31

www.ingramcontent.com/pod-product-compliance
Lightning Source LLC
Chambersburg PA
CBHW051815230426
43672CB00012B/2748